Praise for *Exposure*

"*Exposure* invites readers through the backstory of one determined sociologist who proves herself an insightful instigator of new, informed feminist perspectives of the porn industry. A respected outsider-turned-insider, Dr. Chauntelle's engaging story is a porn nerd jackpot that academia would be wise to add to its syllabus."
—Jiz Lee, performer and editor of *Coming Out Like a Porn Star*

"Almost everything written about the pornography industry has come from outsiders, and much of that writing caricatures the enterprise. *Exposure* offers a unique and fresh view of the adult industry through Dr. Chauntelle's unprecedented access to it. This is a groundbreaking book filled with insights into a previously hidden world."
—Ronald Weitzer, PhD, George Washington University

"With a storyteller's voice and a sociologist's eye, Dr. Chauntelle takes readers on a romp behind the scenes of the US adult industry. Tales of her personal experiences in the commercial sex industry put a human face on a cultural landscape that is otherwise rife with stereotypes. This book is both a fly-on-the-wall account and an analytical peek behind the complex and sometimes harsh realities of a business where fantasy rules. Readers will come away from *Exposure* with a better understanding of an often misunderstood industry and a fresh perspective on the business of marketing and selling sex."
—Dr. Kathryn Hausback Korgan, co-author of *The State of Sex*

"These days, there are many academics willing to try their hands at studying the adult porn industry. All too often they have hidden agendas of finding out the 'real reason' women are willing to have sex on camera, or perhaps to 'save' the women's 'souls,' or simply because they're titillated by the idea of getting close to people who have sex for a living. But then there's Dr. Chauntelle, a genuine researcher who isn't afraid to step through the doors of adult businesses, spend time on adult movie sets, and engage with the people who make this multi-billion-dollar industry run. Kudos to her for writing this extremely informative volume!"
—Mark Kernes, Senior Editor for Legal Affairs, AVN Media Network

"The porn industry distrusts interlopers just as much as it craves validating acceptance, or simple tolerance. Why? Because so many writers neglect the complexity behind the narcissism and ridiculousness that porn often embodies, going for a quick joke or quicker dismissal rather than sitting with the array of choices that make up a porn career. Dr. Chauntelle approaches porn with the respect it deserves, not shying from its flaws and giving its workers credit for having made—and living with—difficult decisions. She approaches her subjects as people who've made decisions rather than people who've spun around to find something has happened to them, and that's the great difference in Dr. Chauntelle's work."

—Gram Ponante, Editor of Porn Valley Observed
and Gamelink's Naked Truth

"Some years ago, when I was writing a column for MSNBC and reporting my book, *America Unzipped: The Search for Sex and Satisfaction*, a source suggested I call a 'very smart young woman in Texas' who was studying the world of adult entertainment. In the years since, Dr. Chauntelle has never failed to impress me with her insight and honesty about a world many regard as the ragged, pop-culture stepchild best left in the attic."

—Brian Alexander, author of *America Unzipped:*
The Search for Sex and Satisfaction

"Dr. Chauntelle has written the first insightful book about the 'real' modern adult film industry and world of porn. It's an unbiased and fair examination of the everyday work in porn without prejudices and perceptions. No one else has the combination of academic background and inside knowledge."

—Karen Tynan, attorney at law and counsel to
adult industry companies and performers

"Dr. Chauntelle's vivid and incisive account of being an outsider looking in on the porn world will change the way you think about the sex industry. It's sharply written and occasionally hilarious, but it's also a sobering reflection on a stigmatized yet rapidly changing industry. For anyone with a passing interest in porn—and let's be honest, we all have more than a passing interest in porn—this book is a must-read."

—EJ Dickson, Lifestyle Editor, TheDailyDot

"Dr. Chauntelle is a wildly innovative public sociologist who turned her own alienation from mainstream academia into an insightful, funny, and smart account of doing research in the marginalized topic of porn. *Exposure* presents the true-to-life story of her own experiences researching the porn industry, providing a complex, rigorous, and honest look into the life of a researcher. She weaves a sociologically sound study of the porn industry with a down-to-earth approach, accessible to both academics and the general public interested in learning more about research practice and the porn industry."
—Corinne Reczek, PhD, Assistant Professor, Departments of Sociology and Women's, Gender, and Sexuality Studies, The Ohio State University

"If 50 *Shades of Grey*, Mark Twain, Larry Flynt, and Stephen Hawking had a baby, she would've been named Chauntelle Tibbals. The good doctor has achieved laser-point accuracy as to how we think and interact when it comes to sex, intimacy, and social behavior. She's a true innovator, having carved her own unique lane of study, point of view, and service to the world. She's friendly, accessible, funny, and a brilliant scholar, with insights and skill sets that are both intriguing and highly necessary."
—Chris Denson, host of the "Innovation Crush" podcast

"A humanizing, thoughtful look at the adult entertainment industry from someone who has spent more than a decade getting to know the people who work in it."
—Nadine Strossen, John Marshall Harlan II Professor of Law, New York Law School, and former president, American Civil Liberties Union

"Porn has become such a pervasive cultural force that it demands to be written about thoughtfully and seriously. Dr. Chauntelle is the sociologist doing just that."
—Vince Mancini, FilmDrunk/UPROXX

"As a long-time member of the adult entertainment community, it's refreshing to see our world examined by a trained professional who didn't come here with preconceived notions of the people who inhabit it. Dr. Chauntelle's honest investigation into the truth of our lives is a welcome change from the usual attitude of 'Pornography: Threat or menace?'

That Dr. Chauntelle had to push back against her department and lost funding and support for wanting to study our world is, sadly, an all-too common story. That she persevered in the face of such fierce resistance is a testament to her vision, hard work, and determination—the product of which you're holding in your hands.

Thank you, Dr. Chauntelle, for being a voice of reason and knowledge rising above the cacophony of bias, ignorance, fear, and mistrust that usually accompanies any discussion of the role of adult entertainment in wider society, as well as the lived experiences of those who work to bring it to life.

If you want to speak from understanding and not parrot media portrayals of porn, read this book!"

—Nina Hartley, award-winning adult entertainment actress
and author of *Nina Hartley's Guide to Total Sex*

"Whether you're already a fan of adult entertainment, curious about its inner workings, or just looking for an inspirational story of one woman's endeavor to bring social justice to a marginalized part of society, Dr. Chauntelle's *Exposure* will grab you with its charm and win you over with its heart.

Equal parts style and substance, this engaging, insightful, and refreshingly honest take on an often-polarizing industry is as entertaining as it is informative. Dr. Chauntelle brings a conversational style of writing to *Exposure* that makes for a breezy read that will have you feeling as if you're sitting across from her at your local coffee shop.

Through her dedicated research, critical thinking, and a special knack for connecting with the personalities in her field of study, Dr. Chauntelle shines a spotlight on a largely misunderstood community and creates important work that will stand the test of time."

—Dan Miller, Managing Editor, XBIZ

"*Exposure* is a humorous and compelling story of a modern woman looking to dispel the common narrative that modern-day pornography is an evil influence on the hearts and minds of our generation. Dr. Chauntelle incessantly pokes holes in the doctrine that most of us in America have grown up with: Sex is not to be enjoyed and sex for pleasure or entertainment is evil, sad, and a last resort for immoral people. *Exposure* shatters those notions."

—Steven St. Croix, eleven-time AVN Award best actor winner

"Dr. Chauntelle brings a voice of expertise and legitimacy to an industry that rarely, if ever, gets the serious treatment it deserves. Her perspective, as a sociologist looking at the adult industry, will enlighten both the curious outsider and the longtime insider. Fighting through the discrimination of the academic community and puritanical myths about sex to become the leading voice of the realities of sexuality in the twenty-first century is a testament to her determination and abilities. I can only hope that her voice reaches more people so that we as a society may have a more informed discourse on sexuality and everything that goes along with it."

—Nate Glass, founder and owner of Takedown Piracy

EXPOSURE

A SOCIOLOGIST EXPLORES
SEX, SOCIETY, and
ADULT ENTERTAINMENT

— xxx —

DR. CHAUNTELLE TIBBALS

With a Foreword by *HUSTLER*'s Theresa Flynt

GREENLEAF
BOOK GROUP PRESS

An abbreviated version of Chapter 14 appeared on MensHealth.com in August 2014.

Chapter 16 is an adaptation of portions of "When Law Moves Quicker Than Culture: Key Jurisprudential Regulations Shaping the US Adult Content Production Industry" in *The Scholar: St. Mary's Law Review on Race and Social Justice* 15 (2013).

Published by Greenleaf Book Group Press
Austin, Texas
www.gbgpress.com

Distributed by Greenleaf Book Group

For ordering information or special discounts for bulk purchases, please contact Greenleaf Book Group at PO Box 91869, Austin, TX 78709, 512.891.6100.

Design and composition by Greenleaf Book Group and Kim Lance
Cover design by Greenleaf Book Group and Kim Lance
Cover image by Roman Samokhin/iStock Collection/Thinkstock

Publisher's Cataloging Publication Data is available.

ISBN: 978-1-62634-193-7

Part of the Tree Neutral® program, which offsets the number of trees consumed in the production and printing of this book by taking proactive steps, such as planting trees in direct proportion to the number of trees used: www.treeneutral.com

TreeNeutral

Printed in the United States of America on acid-free paper

15 16 17 18 19 20   10 9 8 7 6 5 4 3 2 1

First Edition

Other Edition(s):
eBook ISBN: 978-1-62634-194-4

This book is dedicated to my family,
both given and chosen.

Infinite thanks are also due to all those who
have let me spy on them over the years.

Contents

Preface

THERE ARE MANY DIMENSIONS TO EXPOSURE: TO REVEAL something hidden, to lay something bare, to be influenced by something new. You, dear reader, are about to be exposed to one of the most significant subcultures shaping our modern world. You are about to look into a community that's simultaneously influential and reviled, powerful and stigmatized—all through my eyes. *Exposure: A Sociologist Explores Sex, Society, and Adult Entertainment* is my attempt to share only some of my hilarious, ridiculous, occasionally heartbreaking, often challenging, and always enlightening adventures as a sociologist embedded in the world of adult entertainment, or porn.

I began exploring this world in the early 2000s. From content production to occupational safety, from individual proclivities to the wider social implications of commercial sex work—if it has to do with porn, I'm in it. I love my work for many reasons, reasons that have everything to do with the amazing people I've met, the stereotypes I've helped shatter, and the opportunities I've been given for personal growth.

Over the years, my sociological endeavors have provided me with endless fun. I've had many fascinating encounters, research based and otherwise, and the day-to-day is never mundane. Consequently, these stories are also pretty fun—amusing dalliances and surprising tales from inside a mysterious business. But they're also more than *just* that. The experiences in these chapters are stories from my daily life—lessons I've learned from things that have actually happened. They're a significant part of my own evolution, both as a scholar and as a human being. All that, and they help further my work, too.

Like it or not, adult entertainment is a hugely influential component of our culture. It plays a part in shaping who we are as a society. And we as a society help shape it right back. Porn is informed by our sexual desires and dreams, often in ways that we're uncomfortable with. That's where I come in. Through my (mis)adventures, I hope you will discover new ways to think about porn and adult entertainment . . . and maybe even your own life.

It's all entertaining and enjoyable, and—most important—it's all a learning experience.

Foreword

BY THERESA FLYNT

Sexy, passionate, and erotic . . . or obscene, filthy, and immoral?

Depending on whether you are for or against it, these are words often used to describe the adult entertainment industry. The words *cultural, significant,* and *educational* are less common descriptions . . . until now. Thanks to Dr. Chauntelle Tibbals and other proponents, people are beginning to look at the adult industry as a key cultural component of our society. It's a space that both reflects our world and comes from it. After all, as the Romans demonstrated in their regard for sexual expression, our forms of entertainment say a lot about our culture. Porn and erotic content are no different.

In *Exposure,* Chauntelle offers fascinating insight into the adult industry's inner workings, from film sets to business operations. She offers readers the chance to explore a mysterious world through her eyes—the eyes of an informed, sex-positive, empowered woman. But as interesting as her accounts are, I found myself drawn even more to the plight she has endured in order to be taken seriously by another peer group—researchers and academics. Though criticized by scholars in the university system, Chauntelle persevered. Her work now helps to validate the importance of analyzing and understanding all outsiders—because all communities, even the marginalized ones, contribute to society overall. *Exposure* is a testament to this.

Chauntelle has made some waves to challenge existing stereotypes and misconceptions about sex and adult entertainment. I am very familiar with and appreciative of her fight, not only for porn's right to exist in our society but also for the recognition of its value and contributions. The study of adult entertainment helps us become more in tune with our own sexuality as we, at our core, are all sexual beings.

Introduction

WORST. MEETING. EVER.

IT WAS A MISTY-RAINY SPRING DAY IN AUSTIN, TEXAS. Everything was warm and wet and blossom scented, and people were driving even worse than usual. The cityscape whipped past me, not really registering, as I forced myself to knuckle down and concentrate on the task at hand. Although it wasn't my first time down this road, the pressure of this particular day had scrambled my general calm. My heart was racing, and my chest was heaving. My quads screamed, and my lungs burned as my ass bounced in time with every push forward. As I made what was nowhere near my last liquid-lightening left-hand turn through a busy intersection, I felt my back tire skid. I thought briefly about getting a helmet. For an instant, I rethought my flip-flops.

But my bike was my friend, and I wasn't going to crash. I would make it to campus. I would make it to my meeting on time.

I was in my first year of a sociology PhD program at the University of Texas at Austin (UT). I had come into the program with a master's degree, which I'd totally thought would make my life easier. Unfortunately, I was kinda wrong.

Because of credits I had earned elsewhere, I was a little further along in the program than most of the other students in my cohort—a fancy way of saying "people who start working on a degree at the same time as you." Consequently, I was already under serious pressure from the person slated to be my advisor to come up with a dissertation research topic.

This whole dissertation research topic thing is a tricky business. At the very least, it's something doctoral students end up basing five or so years of their life on. At the very most, it sets you on a lifelong, career-spanning course of study. And the entire project is guided and shaped and, ultimately, signed off on by one person—your advisor. It's an awfully big commitment, but that's just the way it was (and still is) and "the way it is" is what I had signed up for. The pressure I was experiencing was not unusual for this point in my academic development, save two teeny tiny little details: first, my advisor didn't seem to like the direction I was going, because, second, the direction I was going was toward porn.

I had been racing my bike to campus, wearing flip-flops and no helmet in the rain, because I was on my way to meet my advisor for what seemed like the five hundredth time in the past few weeks. We were going to talk about my research interests and dissertation project ideas. Again. These meetings were getting increasingly tense and—as we batted ideas back and forth—unproductive. So I was already feeling pretty winded and dreadful as I dashed up several flights of stairs to her office.

And it began. "Who cares?" she asked, referring to my proposed topic.

"Everyone!" I said. "Everyone cares about this."

To which she shot me a pointed, incredulous look over the top of her glasses. Not five minutes in, and I was already starting to annoy her. I was wasting her time. I tried again.

"So little is known about this industry, but it makes all this money . . . Surely there's something going on."

She hit me with the same look of incredulity, now faintly peppered with disgust, as she walked over to her wall of books and pulled a few titles of the shelves. Their premises were, essentially, *porn hurts, porn harms,* and *porn is a heterosexist tool for destroying women and strengthening patriarchy through capitalism.* As she slid them toward me, her message was clear: "This is what we know. This is what goes on."

I tried again.

"This industry is legal, it has a history in our society and a place in our culture, but so little is known about it, and it makes all this money. People are watching this stuff. There has to be something going on."

I was repeating myself, and unfortunately I wasn't making much sense. I had been nervous on arrival, and I now was starting to really get flustered. I didn't understand what she was looking for, which was simply a clear statement of a research question or puzzle. But even if I'd had that, what I didn't grasp at the time was that I was up against an impossibility. My advisor had already come to a conclusion about what was going on in porn, and there was no book on her shelves or in the university library or anywhere else that I could use to suggest otherwise.

"'Stuff'?" She wrinkled her nose, shook her head, and turned away from the table where we were seated across from one another. I was dismissed. The meeting was over.

I tried one more time.

"This industry has been around for decades. People claim to hate it, but they consume it like mad. So many people talk about it, but I've been looking into it and no one ever talks to the people actually involved. We don't know anything about them, really. No one goes to where they work or sees what's actually happening in their lives. Nothing can be as completely bad as all those books say. Stuff doesn't work that way. Lots of people, millions even, watch porn, and lots of people work on making it. Doesn't that make it even kind of significant. . . ?"

I trailed off as she oh-so-slowly turned back around. "Why do you care, Chauntelle?"

This took me by surprise. "Huh?" I replied, as inarticulate as could be.

"Why do you care? Why are you interested in this 'stuff'? This 'workplace'?" Her voice was raised slightly, more agitated now than annoyed. I could see the wheels turning in her head as an idea about exactly why I cared began to take shape. She squinted at me just slightly, and I started to feel extremely self-conscious of my blonde pigtails, my Southern California casual clothes, my pierced nose, and my glittery black fingernails. Her office door was open behind me, and other students were waiting in the hall.

"What do you mean?" I asked, frantically searching for a smart-sounding way to say that I was fascinated by this thing that everyone seemed to consume but no one was willing to acknowledge, that I loved the fact that this was an industry filled with rule-breakers, and that I was absolutely electrified by the possibility of exploring something new. I was going to speak to the porn industry, both because it was made up of people who deserved to have their voices heard . . . and because no one else had the guts to.

But I had thrown down the final straw with my last "What do you mean?" She snapped. She came halfway out of her chair, palms flat on the table. "What do I mean? *Why do you want to watch people fucking, Chauntelle?*" she shouted.

Seriously. She shouted.

— x x x —

I have no memory of the remainder of that meeting, no recollection of our final words that day. I have no memory of actually leaving her office, my books and belongings stacked in my arms as I shuffled outside, back into the misty air. I made my way to the bike rack, where I had unceremoniously tossed my ride not thirty minutes earlier. My friend Jordan, who was a student in the same cohort as me, was there, carefully locking up her own bike. She was so much better at this whole living-in-a-place-with-weather thing. She had on rubber-soled shoes and a snazzy helmet.

"Heeeey," she greeted me in her characteristic way. Then quickly: "Are you ok? What's wrong?"

"Dude," I said, all school pretense abandoned, my California-speak completely unchecked. "I think something really bad just happened. . . ."

1

How Did a Nice Girl Like You Get into (Studying) Porn?

I'VE HEARD PEOPLE ASK PERFORMERS A VERSION OF THAT QUESTION countless times: "How did a nice girl like you get into porn?" It sounds like a reasonable thing to ask, complimenting one's niceness and asking after someone's life-so-far story. People's responses are as varied as the performers themselves; however, this question and any number of subsequent responses (if one can get them) are often a little sticky. You see, the rationale behind that initial question is generally not as "I want to learn about you!" as one might think. In fact, more often than not, it's really just a glossy cover for something more along the lines of: "You're too good to be doing this [insert unsavory adjective here] thing, so please tell me what awful series of occurrences cornered you such that you had no other choice." There's usually a good measure of "Your choices make me uncomfortable" thrown in there, too.

As I worked my way inside the adult entertainment industry, I began to realize that these types of questions and the viewpoints behind them were born largely out of misinformation. I also realized rather quickly that these misinformed viewpoints applied to me, too. I was not immune to their application, nor am I impervious to their effects today. I am a sociologist and a scholar. I earned my PhD from one of the top research universities in the United States. When I began exploring the adult industry, I did not have one single contact in the business. I had never engaged in a sex work occupation, nor had any of my friends or associates. (At least, not to my knowledge.)

In the beginning, all I knew was that it seemed like many people had opinions about porn. Some unabashedly loved it. They followed industry politics and personalities and spent money on products and whatnot. Others enjoyed the industry privately, and often secretly, while simultaneously feeling somewhat ashamed. And then there were the folks who opposed porn at all costs, with unparalleled passion and conviction. For some reason, regardless of the specifics, porn inspired very strong emotions in lots of people. Though it was just a gut feeling, I knew there was something bigger going on from the day I started looking at the industry. I had no idea what it was at the time.

And that's really it, the entire overview of my initial interest in adult entertainment. All of it. The end. But I still got the question, "Why is a nice girl like you studying porn?" I still get it to this day. So here are the ins and outs of how and why.

— x x x —

My life course leading up to today, or even to that meeting I was talking about earlier, was long and winding but no more so than anyone else's. I'm pretty regular, advantaged even—an able-bodied, decently smart, white person living in the United States. Thinking about it, minus the woman part and minus my decidedly "unclassy" habitus,[1] I'd actually say I'm more advantaged than regular. And though I know it's trendy these days to focus on everyone's unique snowflake qualities, I'm only rare in one way really: I was raised in Los Angeles. Not in the city proper but throughout the entire sprawl that is the greater LA metropolitan, suburban, and outlying areas. So were both my parents.

They're a crafty duo, those two—and important to this story. Outliers and outsiders themselves, my mom and dad employed all kinds of tricky tactics to make sure my brothers and I grew up to be outliers and outsiders as well. Everything about my upbringing was rowdy, and my parents seemed to take great delight in cultivating rowdiness in us kids. They found the last place in LA County close enough to the city to travel to work but still technically in the middle of nowhere to raise us: Acton, California, a small town near the glorious Antelope Valley Desert of Extreme Nothingness. And out in the middle of nowhere, my family and I did everything from riding motorcycles and horses and firing guns to "camping" in storage sheds and building forts out of bales of hay. It was fun.

My parents had interesting notions about social propriety and child rearing. We arrived to every convivial activity and extended family function twenty minutes early, circled the block fifty times before walking in right on time, and always left before everyone else. As kids, my brothers and I were all given a decently rigorous set of rules, standards, and expectations to abide by, and no deviations were tolerated. When we misbehaved, punishments were clever and effective. For example, one time, after we had snuck out in the middle of the night and gone swimming in a neighbor's irrigation tank, my parents dropped us off at a local community church for a couple of hours. Apparently, there was no greater punishment than having to interact with an organized group of people who seemed to be the opposite of outsiders.

By the time I was an early adolescent, the whole "stand alone" (or at least "stand with your family and buddies outside the big group") thing was definitely working. From who my friends were to the cultural and social things I found alluring, my need to be off the beaten path was almost compulsive. And, partly because I was such a little instigator, so was my desire to remind everyone who remained on the path that outsiders were people, too.

But I also had my eye on getting out of the desert and into college. Consequently, I—the little rebel—did all sorts of oxymoronic-seeming things. I held several offices in high school leadership, the only kid with purple hair. I was also the only purple-haired member of the track team and the only kid in every AP and honors class with a collection of fairly aggressive concert T-shirts. And because I was still just a bratty teen, I did all sorts of obnoxious things, too, like being the only kid who blatantly ditched those same AP and honors classes on an excessively regular basis. Or rallying relentlessly to have "my" music, which actually belonged to a lot of other kids in school too, played during pep rallies. (It was only fair that everyone's tastes were reflected, right?) When I lost that battle, I sneakily did it anyway.

As I made my way into college at UCLA, my outright brattiness mellowed while my need to push boundaries and champion folks with relatively marginalized voices matured and refined. For example, I was a reporter for the *Daily Bruin* in the late nineties. I had to beat out several other student writers to get a spot on the roster, and it was fun to get to go to different events on campus, things that my scrubby self never would've been welcome at otherwise. In those days, I had a good friend who was really into women's rights and feminist politics. I knew nothing about that stuff, but I became intrigued and started going to Women's Resource Center (WRC)–sponsored events with her. And after attending a few of these gut-wrenching occasions where students discussed various forms of social marginalization, physical abuse, and the like, something dawned on me. These were important moments in campus culture, and *there was no one from the* Daily Bruin *there!* I mean, I was there, but I was there as an attendee, not a reporter.

When I went to my editor with this news, I was mortified to learn that no reporter was ever assigned to WRC events because, I was told, no one was interested in all that feminist stuff. So I started covering it. And because it was still the late nineties and gender and sexuality were lumped together in a relatively uncritical way, I started covering the LGB (there was no T or Q in the acronym then, at least not at UCLA) events, too. In those days, I didn't really understand most of the politics or issues, I just knew that certain groups on campus— outliers and outsiders—were not being included in the student news voice. It was like these members of the community didn't even exist, which gave me all the reason I needed to jump in and do whatever I could to change that. Plus, let's be honest: I also thought it might piss some people off.

After I completed my over-amped undergraduate education at UCLA in 2000, I found myself not knowing how *not* to be in school. I was a whopping twenty-two years old and in the middle of a pretty significant identity crisis, so I decided to enroll in a terminal master's program at Cal State Northridge (CSUN). A master's degree in sociology? Sure, why not? I had to bide my time while I worked on finding myself.

As it happens, CSUN was (and still is) located right smack in the middle of Porn Valley, a slightly snarky nickname for the San Fernando Valley, which is yet another piece of the giant Los Angeles city-sprawl. A little background is in order.

People have been creating various forms of sexually explicit content in the US since the early 1900s; however, because "smut" was both vaguely defined and pretty unlawful back then, any production of this type of material was fairly clandestine. Then, in the 1950s, some key court cases made things a little less illegal by providing a clearer working definition of obscenity. Ever so slowly, individuals interested in creating sexually explicit content came out of the woodwork. As the years passed, an informal collection of somewhat interconnected folks began creating elaborate short film projects that featured depictions of some form of hardcore sex. By the 1970s, people were creating full-length films that focused on sex-specific narratives.

For various reasons, members of the nascent porn industry moved from the East Coast to San Francisco and Los Angeles during the 1970s. Over time, content production in the San Francisco Bay Area became more of a part-time artistic and political endeavor (at least, for many of the performers), while businesses in LA began to resemble a conventional industry. By the 1980s, LA's San Fernando Valley had become porn's absolute epicenter. And today, though the industry is constantly changing and though there's plenty of adult content production that occurs in the Bay Area, across the US, and around the world, Porn Valley is still the center of the smut universe.

I recall being dimly aware of the Valley's reputation as the *other* Hollywood when I started at CSUN, but that reputation held no real relevance for me as I directed my energies toward graduate work. I had a lot of classes to take; and, because I had taken so much hard science at UCLA (I was a double major: physiological sciences and sociology), I decided I would go for what was really interesting to me—gender and sex stuff, with some additional focus on the social phenomena of work and organizing thrown in for good measure.

As I began to delve into more nuanced areas of sociology and—*gasp!*—feminist scholarship, I realized pretty quickly that sex work, particularly sex work in porn production, had a contentious history in academic, feminist, and activist worlds. I learned about the polarizing "porn wars," which generally broke down to *either* porn is wholly awful *or* porn is just mostly awful, with the exception of some niche exploratory genres. I found myself getting pretty wrapped up in the whole "porn is bad (at least mostly)" thing.

But while all this was happening through books and in classes, there were other things happening in real life, too. Over the course of many long hours and late nights working, studying, and socializing, the mysterious adult industry began to reveal itself in subtle ways. Sometimes it was in the form of billboards advertising various events at local strip clubs; other times, ads in the *LA XPress*, which I had begun flipping through regularly when I was still an undergrad. Sometimes it was in the form of coworkers—guys, of course—losing it in the restaurant where I worked because some big-deal performer was dining in their section. And sometimes it was in the form of rather … umm … noticeable people standing in line at the local Starbucks. They had to be porn people, right? Why else would they be dressed like that at 11 a.m.?

I'm naturally nosy and have always been an unabashed people-watcher, two sociologist's skills in the raw, so, of course, I became intrigued. Who were these people working in this mostly, supposedly morally reprehensible (at least according to my schoolbooks) industry, degrading women and warping people's ideas about sex while drinking lattes near my school? Such were the stereotypes informing my thinking at the time. I found it odd that no one else around me seemed to notice or care. The apparently harmonious, albeit often unacknowledged, existence between "regular people" and "porn people" fascinated me, particularly given the adult industry's fairly negative reputation. I became even more interested and began to do a little investigating.

I learned that at the time in the United States it was only legal to produce porn in the state of California (now it's only legal in California and New Hampshire) and that most of the world's porn was made by a large cluster of companies operating mere miles from CSUN. What's more, many adult personalities and performers had written autobiographical accounts of their experiences in the business. People cared enough to write books about this stuff!

I became obsessed with the stories of former adult performers Linda Lovelace and Jerry Butler, as well as with the legendary tragedies and horrors associated with Savannah, Traci Lords, and John C. Holmes. There were some impressive legal battles, too—for example, that of Philip D. Harvey, the co-founder of Adam & Eve, a mail-order company specializing in sex-related products and rooted in public health that has been prosecuted multiple times by the US federal and various state governments—and some instances of porn performers poking their heads up into the mainstream à la Ginger Lynn Allen.

Somewhere in the midst of my rabid consumption of all these available stories, I began to wonder: Surely everything couldn't possibly be so dramatic? Surely not everyone commits suicide (Savannah), dates Hollywood bad boys (Ginger Lynn Allen), is in an abusive personal relationship (Linda Lovelace), gets busted by the feds (Philip D. Harvey), or is linked to one of the most gruesome massacres in Hollywood history (John C. Holmes and 1981's Wonderland murders)? Surely, out of all the people working in this industry, there had to be some "normal" folks living "normal" lives, right? Where was all the information about them? Where were all the other stories?

It was as if the real meat of the industry was being hidden or kept secret. It was as if the people involved were concentrated into some sort of porn bubble that enabled them to live, work, and contribute to wider society while simultaneously isolating them from it. I was absolutely captivated by this mysterious dynamic, compelled by what appeared to be an almost schizophrenic desire to both consume and reject porn in US culture. And I was totally part of this at-odds juxtaposition—simultaneously horrified by what seemed to be happening and fascinated by what I instinctively felt had to be more complex. I was eager to explore the processes that had contributed to this bubble, but this industry and whatever phenomena were responsible for shaping it were far too big for a master's program.

I was gonna have to get a PhD. So I got to work on that.

I finished up my master's degree at CSUN in 2003 and eventually moved on to the doctoral program in sociology at UT in 2004. I hit the ground running as soon as school started that fall and began exploring anti-porn activism in the US during a history seminar my very first semester. I also started learning a lot more about research methods, which caused me to notice something seriously suspect: The vast majority of the "porn is mostly awful" literature I had been swallowing whole while at CSUN was rather methodologically unsound.[2]

Discussions of "violent" or "misogynist" content engaged only small, unsubstantiated, and cherry-picked selections of fairly dated material. There were no sampling frames (itemized lists of those surveyed or studied and/or of every case possibly surveyed or studied) to be had, and nothing was even remotely close to representative. Many of the sweeping conclusions and arguments made in opposition of porn read more along the lines of "This is bad because I don't like it!" rather than "I have demonstrated through A, B, and C that XXX is...." And perhaps most egregiously, no one ever seemed to talk to anyone who actually worked in this industry; or, if they did, it was always to the same handful of players who'd had bad experiences. I had done ethnography[3] work in restaurants to complete my MA, and I had spoken to a bunch of waitresses and servers in the process. Talking to people who were actually doing what it was that one was studying made sense to me, and those porn-free assessments of porn were starting to look a little suspicious on the basis of methods alone.

Then I read Lynn Chancer's *Reconcilable Differences*. (It was on the required reading list for a course on gender and sexuality I was taking in 2005. Ironically, this course was being taught by the same professor/advisor who would later demand to know why I wanted to watch people fucking.) In this book, Chancer takes on many divisive topics—things that people generally feel one way or the other about: beauty, "victim" versus "survivor," prostitution, and porn. Chancer's main point on every topic and in the book as a whole is that nothing—absolutely nothing—is all good or all bad. Instead, according to Chancer, most things are *both* good *and* bad. *Reconcilable Differences* is a brilliant call to arms away from either/or scholarship in lieu of both/and considerations.

I was completely in agreement with this both/and concept; as were, it seemed, all fifteen or so of my classmates. But when we got to discussing the porn chapter in class, one young woman became absolutely outraged. She asserted, with passion and conviction, that both/and considerations were not applicable in this case. Porn was, in fact, objectively bad. It harmed women and men in myriad ways, and it corrupted people's humanity. When pressed on her stance though, she couldn't explain why. She had never spoken to anyone who had ever worked in the adult entertainment industry, and she could see the methodological and epistemological problems embedded in the all-or-nothing "truth" she was touting. But none of this mattered. This person, who had to be at least a little bit rational and bright by virtue of her place as a student at the university, couldn't separate what she felt and thought (which was real and valid and her right) from the possibility that others might see things differently, that there may be other experiences and versions of reality operating somewhere out in the ether.

I had never actually seen this sort of thing in person before. I had never seen a person come totally unglued over porn in this way, especially not someone in a graduate-level classroom. It was amazing. Porn was capable of making people lose their common sense, analytic skills, and composure. It could scramble the smartest, most educated of brains. And that was it for me. I was hooked—porn for life. But I had absolutely no idea what specifically about porn for life I wanted to explore. *All of it!* was what I was thinking, but that definitely wouldn't fly within the strictures of graduate school. It was around this time that I started having all those meetings with my advisor, and you already know how that went. . . .

After that fateful spring day and that fateful spring meeting, things really changed for me. It was subtle at first. My advisor wouldn't respond to my e-mails, and it became impossible to connect with her during her office hours. A gnawing feeling began to grow in my stomach, but I convinced myself she was just dealing with end-of-the-semester obligations. But when I didn't get funding for the summer, not panicking became a little bit more difficult. There weren't a lot of positions available during that particular term, and it only made sense that they'd go to students who were farther along in the program, right? I was pretty far along, but I didn't get funded. And I still couldn't get a response from my advisor.

The other shoe dropped pretty hard soon after. I found out that I, a second-year student who had made good progress and was one year away from taking comprehensive exams (so I was really more like a third-year student), didn't have funding for the fall either.[4] That's when I realized the severity of what had happened at that meeting in the spring. And, to add insult to injury, the sociology department didn't tell me about any of this until just before the semester began— far too late for me to find another position in a different division of the university (not that those were easy to come by either, mind you).

The stress of this—thousands of dollars' worth of out-of-state tuition due *now*, a full load of graduate-level classes looming, no job, and no health insurance—was almost too much. After twenty-four hours of panicking, crying, and vowing revenge, I did the only thing I could. I formulated Plan B. I took out an emergency loan (the university was happy to sign me over to a large national bank), I got a job serving cocktails in a raucous downtown bar, and I barged my way onto the adjunct faculty of the local community college. I already had a couple years' worth of college-level teaching experience in California, which luckily was enough to get me a course assignment at a satellite campus thirty miles north. It wasn't much, but it was something.

I scraped together a semblance of financial stability relatively quickly, but there was one other thing: UT allegedly had this strange noncompete clause stating that if you had "other funding" (read: worked at a bar and taught a community college class that paid a sum total of about $2,000 over the course of four months—four whopping $500 installments), it would lower your chances of getting tuition support from them. Why would they pay you when someone else was? But I *needed* to get funding from the university. I needed the insurance and (at least) the fee reduction. But mostly, I needed the myriad intangible things that came from being let back into the fold with all my peers.

So I kept my jobs a secret, especially the teaching one. Then the rumors began: Chauntelle wants to study porn, so she must have some connection to porn. Chauntelle lost her funding because of porn, so she must be *doing* porn . . . or at least stripping? When a kind and concerned professor I had worked with during my first year told me about these rumors over lunch one day, more to see if I was okay than anything else, I was caught between laughing myself silly and a rage so acute it burned a hole through my soul. Really? That's all I could do, strip or fuck? Working in either one of those occupations takes craft and skill. Neither is shameful or a laughing matter. But the fact that these "shameful" occupations were all I could do in the eyes of my scholarly peers. . . . Well, that bothered me. It was a difficult time.

Oddly enough, this unfortunate series of circumstances fueled my passion for porn like Santa Ana winds on a Southern California wildfire—intensely. What possibly could be happening in Porn Valley that warranted all of this nonsense? Better, what did people imagine was happening? I was going to find out. And I would not be beaten.

At this point, I came up with two primary objectives. First, to research porn and the adult industry. I needed to get to a point where I had enough information to articulate, clearly and succinctly, what I suspected was worthy of scholarly consideration. I also figured that I needed to learn more basics about the industry so I wouldn't sound like a total poseur when I finally got the opportunity to speak to someone who was directly involved. Second, I had to find a new advisor. This was imperative because, as I said before, your advisor basically shapes and controls your entire graduate school experience. But finding one was not going to be an easy task. I had already been tagged as belonging to my first advisor, and no one was signing up for her sloppy seconds.

It took about a year and some serious networking, but I eventually found a new person to work with—a wonderful and supportive yet endlessly challenging, giving, and passionate woman who singlehandedly grew my brain in ways that I still cannot begin to fully appreciate or articulate. My work and my life are better because of her, the absolute embodiment of a true mentor and friend. So in that respect, it all worked out.

Approximating how the adult industry worked from distant Texas, however, took a bit more doing. I spent about one year on background research—late nights bogged down with dial-up Internet, reading, referencing, and cross-referencing industry trade publications, blogs, and retail websites, along with the occasional mainstream news article. I was trying to build a remote picture from the ground up, and it was very slow going. Eventually, I came up with something sociology-worthy to look at: the expansion of women's rights in the absence of a social movement.[5] Now I just had to figure out a way in.

I knew the San Fernando Valley was an obvious choice for my project, but it had become clear to me that the bubble around the adult industry was thick and tight. Just getting casual access would be a difficult task, and here I was attempting to do a rigorous scholarly study within the confines of university-sanctioned research protocols. Since I still had no connection to the industry, I began working on making contacts. Using information and insights from my background research, I identified four people I thought might develop into useful points of entrée. Each person had worked in the industry for more than twenty years and was directly connected to either a porn production company or a service-provision business with industry-only clientele. After all sorts of snail mail and e-mail outreach, all four agreed to speak with me; and, eventually, three agreed to meet with me in person. So I scheduled a "business trip" back home, one that happened to coincide with spring break.

I recall the first of these meetings vividly. It was my first-ever face-to-face interaction with "porn people." I was meeting with a company's CEO and production executive armed only with my little bit of background research and wrestling with every negative feminist and culturally informed stereotype imaginable. I was a nervous wreck. When I arrived at their main office, which was located in the most innocuous-looking commercial building ever, I paused in my car for a long moment. I might have been hyperventilating. What might be going on inside this building? What was I about to do? Was I about to be morally corrupted? Kidnapped? Coerced into something "deviant"? Would these "pornographers" be able to see how nervous (and, truthfully, how frightened) I was? How I actually knew absolutely nothing about their industry or their lives? Moreover, was I about to offend working people with my head-in-the-clouds academic desire to "study" them? After what felt like an eternity of self-reflection, I entered the building . . .

. . . where I was greeted by a cheerful pretty secretary and offered a seat in a perfectly bland reception area. I felt disoriented and a little dizzy. I'm not sure what I was expecting, but it certainly wasn't the lobby at my dentist's office. After a few moments of waiting, I was led behind some closed doors to a corporate meeting room decorated with giant posters of glamorous ladies in lingerie and a massive case housing a large number of gold and Lucite statuettes. There I met a sharp, intense man in his early forties and a smiling friendly woman, also in her early forties. We sat around one end of a giant table and started talking. Our subsequent hour-long conversation, I feel, marked the actual beginning of my learning about the realities of adult production. Everything I had done so far was nothing compared to what I learned in that one face-to-face exchange. Needless to say, my other meetings were less stressful.

I followed up these springtime consultations a couple months later by doing what every college student does—I went home for the summer. I spent six weeks in LA developing additional contacts and strengthening rapport with people in the adult business. By the time

I headed back to Texas for the fall, I had networked with all sorts of women and men at various industry trade and social events and had developed many strong connections. I was always forthcoming and fully disclosed my identity as a graduate student/researcher to anyone I had more than a passing conversation with. I still had comprehensive exams to take and a dissertation proposal to write, but I finally felt like things were starting to come together.

—— x x x ——

Sometimes, ideas that look great and make sense on paper don't quite follow the script when you try to apply them in the real world. This is pretty much exactly what happened with my field research. At the time of my dissertation proposal defense, I planned to explore my research questions (about women's rights expansion in the absence of a social movement) with a mixed-methodological approach combining comparative historical-informed sociology, in-depth interviews, and adult film content analysis. I was going to conduct the interviews over the course of eight weeks, which meant that I got to go home for another summer.

I went back to LA and immediately set up my first interview with one of my strongest contacts in the industry, a very well-known content producer. After some preliminary chitchat that blossomed into a great talk about the ins and outs of the company, I was presented with an unheard-of opportunity: I was offered an unpaid summer "internship" in their public relations department. I was to assist this company's PR representative with mailings, media archival updating, and other similar projects for approximately twenty hours per week. In exchange for my work, I would be able to observe the inner workings of the company, interact with other employees on a daily basis, and attend any events, shows, and so on that occurred during my time there. After some consideration (which really amounted to me feeling spastically anxious and excited) and a couple long talks with my advisor (who told me to calm down and focus), I went for it.

During those weeks, I worked in an actual porn production office. I mailed things, photocopied things, carried things, answered phones, stacked cartons and crates, drove people places, ran around, and did pretty much every other flunky job you can imagine. The best was the week I was tasked with spray-painting promotional boxes for a reissued classic film—two hundred boot-size boxes outside in an alley during the dead of San Fernando Valley summer heat, to be exact. It was the opposite of glamorous and not at all sexy, but it was fun to do something other than type and teach. I also got to attend a fan show and a couple of industry trade events (business-only things), and I got to go onto sets. Yes, sets—where porn was being made and sex was being had. I talked to everyone I could, conducted informal interviews whenever possible, soaked up every bit of information possible, and took endless notes. As before, I told everyone I was an intern and a researcher. Some people were intrigued, but most couldn't have cared less. This "data-gathering" period informed a major portion of my dissertation and helped me build a foundation for my future endeavors—exploring the adult industry's sociocultural significance.

A lot happened to me and around me and (sometimes) because of me, both during my days as a porn intern and during the years it took me to earn my PhD. Ironically though, one of the most significant things to happen was actually something that *didn't*—I never got my funding back. I had to piece together survival money very suddenly in 2005, and those first panicked steps really shaped the rest of my time in graduate school. While most of my peers were holed up in offices

down the hallway from one another, rubbing elbows with faculty, networking at symposia, eating free lunches and drinking free cocktails,
and getting "writing grants"[6] from any number of benevolent programs (within the university and beyond), I was busy holding down
anywhere from two to four part- and full-time jobs. There was not a
lot of time for hobnobbing, which had an extremely negative impact
on the integrated, network-based dimensions of my academic career.

During the years I was in graduate school, I worked as a college
professor in three different university systems and in several higher
education coordination positions. I also worked at about one hundred
other odd jobs, which included, but were not limited to, serving drinks
at a bar, under-the-table restaurant and catering work, working as an
online sociology instructor, ghostwriting and editing (something I
still do to this day), door-to-door data collection for the United States
Census, mentoring and tutoring "advanced" students at one university and "ordinary" students at another, reading and evaluating others' funding and grant proposals, and data coding for others' research
projects. And I did all this while taking classes, passing comprehensive
exams, developing a research project, doing fieldwork, gathering data,
and writing a dissertation. I was tired a lot, but somehow, in spite of
what often felt like impossible (and impossibly unfair) circumstances,
I ended up finishing my degree, paying my bills, and having a much
more interesting time than I imagine most people do.

2

Disco Dolls in Hot Skin

I CAN REMEMBER THE FIRST PORN I EVER SAW.

Growing up pre-Internet as I did, the first thing I came across that might have been porn was scrambled cable television stuff that I accidentally got peeks of while channel surfing for heavy metal videos and episodes of *My So-Called Life*. I say "might have been" because you could always see just enough to know there was something naked going on but never enough to know exactly what. Given what I now know about adult content and different distribution modes and models today, the snow and squiggles I saw back in the day were probably nothing more than some very lovely softcore.

That was the end, until I began my undergraduate days at UCLA. I am one of those individuals—both blessed and cursed—who began college right when computers were busy transforming society, in 1995. But things were still in flux back then. So even though students had the opportunity to "attend" virtual office hours (you weren't really attending anything—it just meant a chat room) and everyone technically had an e-mail address, you could survive pretty easily without the World Wide Web. I didn't have my own computer the entire time I was an undergrad, and my Internet experiences were limited to surfing around at the medical library where I worked.

The library had a few employees-only terminals behind the circulation desk and about twenty or so machines with Internet access for patrons' use in the main lobby (quite a novelty at the time). Back then, infectious pop-up windows plagued Internet users. A browsing novice would get one, then another, then another and another, until about a million windows were open, and the screen was frozen solid. This happened with websites of all types, but it happened particularly often with porn. I still wonder if this was because porn sites were more enthusiastic about their pop-ups or if it was because people were just looking at them more frequently. It may have been a combination of both.

Anyway, I would occasionally come upon coworkers looking at porn stills behind the desk, but we all knew enough to avoid locking up the terminals. The patrons, though? Not so much. At least once per shift, some pissed-off medical student or sheepish-looking health professional would need help with the public computers. All of the terminals had been locked up, you see, and rendered unusable by pop-ups. And, more often than not, the pop-ups were from porn sites. One of the library employees would then have to go around to each machine, restarting and resetting them one at a time. Patrons would practically fight over the computers as they opened back up, eager to do whatever they had come to the library for in the first place. And in many instances, that would start the pop-up cycle all over again.

It always made me laugh. Porn—how silly!

The truth is, though, I was scared to death of porn when I was in college (I never really thought about it much before that), but not because I actually knew anything about things that were considered pornographic. I was scared to death of porn because I was scared to death of the socially constructed *idea* of it.

Porn was this mysterious *ick* that I had never truly seen or experienced. And I wasn't about to go looking into it: The channels were all scrambled, and there was always a coworker around. Besides, as a(n alleged) nice young lady, I wasn't supposed to be looking at that stuff in the first place. So I never got a true taste of the actual products porn produced. And I definitely didn't know anyone who would ever condescend to work in such an industry, so there was no one I could ask. At least, no one who actually knew anything.

Back then, my information about porn came from the mainstream media. And in the mainstream news, no discernable distinction was ever made between prostitutes (who were all law-breaking, drugged-out street hookers), exotic dancers (the sleazy and scandalous counterparts of sleazy and scandalous musicians), and porn performers, who apparently were an amalgamation of strippers and the lowest class of working girl. The term "sex work" hadn't yet made it into my university's lexicon, at least not in the classes I was taking, and all you ever heard about was depravity. Unfortunately, I wasn't at the point in life where I understood that "depravity" wasn't universal. So really, what I was afraid of was some intangible, unsubstantiated representation that I'd somehow come to associate with porn. And even though I'd never actually seen any adult content, I was mortified by it.

Case in point: One time, when I was about twenty years old, some friends and I went to watch *Disco Dolls in Hot Skin* (also known as *Blonde Emmanuelle*), a groovy 3D porno from what's known as porn's golden era—1975 to 1983—that was being shown at a movie theater on Sunset Boulevard. Let's be clear: This was no sticky, red-light Pussycat Theater. This mainstream movie house was located in a high-profile, high-rent shopping center alongside a Crunch gym, a Virgin Megastore, and a Wolfgang Puck Café—all late-nineties legit. And though I can't tell you what in the world drew me to this event, I can

tell you that it was 100 percent my idea to go. I was the instigator;
everyone else just came along.

I remember being nervous as soon as we parked the car. Me and
my silly ideas. Me and my big mouth! We bought our tickets and
posed for a picture wearing our goofy 3D glasses in front of a *Hot Skin*
film poster displayed outside the theatre. One of the film's stars was in
attendance. (I want to say it was Bill Margold, though I can't recall for
sure. I had no idea who he was at the time.) He gave a little talk before
the reel started. I don't recollect much of what he said, though I do
remember him mentioning something about his penis having always
been his best friend. The theater was packed, and by now I felt nau-
seous. When the picture finally started, everyone (else) cheered.

The film itself is grainy in my memory. It's a classic—playful and
silly—and the plot didn't make much sense. But maybe that's because
I didn't give it the opportunity to unfold. Though I tried to act rowdy
and bold with my buddies, I squirmed around uncomfortably at the
first hint of sex. And then I remember someone being chased through
what I remember being some sort of house party. The pursuer and the
pursued ran through a kitchen, and in that kitchen, while those people
were dashing by, a man was banging some woman from behind. And,
for some odd reason, he was pushing her face into a bowl of soup.

That's what I remember, and that's when I stood up and left.

I stormed out of the theater and sat on a planter, shaken. *The horror
of that poor woman being violated and humiliated while people just run
by! How degrading to be pushed into soup!* I can remember thinking
something along those lines. I had vaguely noted the film's carefree
tone, its campy slapstick, and any number of what-the-heck-is-the-
point-of-this-silliness 3D porno moments. But those elements slipped
further and further away as my indignation grew. I seethed over what
was being reframed in my mind as a brutal and "depraved" culinary

drown-fuck. The disconnect between my intense reaction and the content itself was something I didn't recognize at the time.

What happened? What prompted me to insist on going to see a film, only to huff my way out partway through? I can only speculate that, because I was so afraid of the "depraved" images that had been pre-planted in my head, I couldn't separate what I was actually seeing from what I'd been conditioned to experience.

This line of thinking didn't magically go away when I went to graduate school.

When I was working on my master's degree at CSUN, obsessing over every bit of adult-industry-related biographical material I could get my hands on, I got sucked into anti-porn rhetoric. I believed, for example, the hype about *Deep Throat* and Linda Lovelace—that hers was a tragic case of a life leveled by pornography and her involvement therein (versus a case of a woman severely impacted by a horrifically abusive spouse). Consequently, even though I hadn't actually watched the film, I remember being mortified by its mere existence.

Because that's what every feminist scholar, budding or otherwise, was *supposed* to feel.

When my day of reckoning finally came and I finally sat down to view that infamous movie, I was already well into my PhD program at UT. By this point, I knew quite a bit more about porn, but I had also been living with these "truths" about *Deep Throat* for years. I was prepared for horror. (Honestly, I didn't even want to watch the film, but I felt like I'd be a hypocrite if I didn't.) I braced myself for the atrocities I'd been reading about for so long: a graphic showcasing of a woman's abused body, horrible bruises, and body-punishing sex.

What I saw instead was a lighthearted, albeit somewhat problematic and confusing, comedy, which amounted to a big lesson in the rules of perception.

There are several key, commonly discussed scenes in *Deep Throat*—Linda's infamous poolside chat with her girlfriend is one. But as I watched that scene, rather than seeing the physical evidence of a severely abused woman, which had been described in multiple books and articles I'd read, I saw one or two bruises on Linda's legs that looked like mild versions of what I get kickboxing at the gym or walking into my coffee table during the middle of the night. Granted, I have no idea how Linda got those faint bruises; however, what I saw did not match the intensity of the descriptions I had read. At all.

I also saw some depictions in the film that scholars and media pundits cite today when discussing the allegedly "extreme" or somehow newfangled sex shown in more contemporary porn. For example, folks talk about anal sex in today's content as if it's some recently developed or newly depicted sex act, but there's an anal scene in *Deep Throat*. And sex toys. Anal sex and sex toys in a movie that was released to the public in 1972, and people talk about these things nowadays as if they're new developments in porn?

In the end, I was almost disappointed to find that everything I'd heard about *Deep Throat* was actually embellished hype. In fact, I'm almost certain that most people who talk about the film have never even watched it. And for those who have, it's an excellent lesson in the ways in which one fixed thing—like a film or a bit of text—can be perceived differently by different people. Basically, I was faced with another *Disco Dolls* situation, a clash between "see" and "supposed to see." But something very different happened with *Deep Throat*: I didn't storm out. I kept watching.

The point of all of this, from *Deep Throat* to *Disco Dolls*, is that there are many larger social structures and strictures shaping the ways in which we, as self-regulating and thinking individuals, perceive the world. This includes multiple messages from myriad sources shaping how we're supposed to see certain things. I finally started to figure this out when I was in my mid-twenties; but on that one particular night when I was still a wee undergraduate, I continued to sit on that planter outside the theater, mortified by what I was supposed to have just seen. Eventually, my friends joined me. They were all grumbling about not getting to watch the rest of the movie.

3

Watching Porn for Science

FOR A WHILE, MY ENCOUNTERS WITH PORN CONTINUED to be limited and sporadic. Even while I was doing my preliminary investigating during my master's program, I never actually sat down and tried to familiarize myself with the adult industry's scope of current offerings. And it wasn't until I was beginning the second year of my doctoral program at UT that it dawned on me that this was weird. If I wanted to figure out what was so mind-bending about porn and include some consideration of adult content in my actual work, I should at least familiarize myself with a good contemporary selection, right?

So sometime in 2005, I decided it was time to really start watching porn.

But where to begin? Obvious and basic seemed to be the answer. Armed only with the same painfully slow dial-up Internet service, I looked on the *Adult Video News* (AVN) charts for the then-hot adult title. *Camp Cuddly Pines Power Tool Massacre* was a screwball take on the slasher film genre featuring some big-deal performers from a major production studio. Sweet! I didn't want to wait for a DVD to come in the mail, and this was well before the days of easy video on demand (at least to my knowledge, and the computer/Internet setup I had then probably couldn't have handled VOD anyway), so I decided I was going to have to purchase a copy in a traditional brick-and-mortar store. Me in a sex shop? This would be a first.

I hopped in my car and headed down a Central Texas highway. There were a series of adult stores nearby, and one of them was bound to have the title I was looking for. I pulled into the first parking lot and immediately had to take a few deep breaths. I was getting nervous, and this was starting to look like the beginning of my own power tool massacre. Imagine:

An ordinarily bold young blonde, now totally out of her element, pulls into a dirt lot filled with beat-up trucks. One buzzing streetlight is shining on the porch entryway, and a couple of dudes are scurrying into and out of the building. She creeps up, hesitates at the door, and then says "Fuck it. . . ."

Inside, there's a bored-looking counter clerk off to the left and a few old-school wooden racks holding a paltry number of DVDs and VHS tapes in the middle of the room. No one seems to care about the content of these racks. All the action is in the back, where three or four guys are waiting for their turn to enter one of a series of doors along the back wall—booths. (As in booths to watch a few minutes of porn and jerk off in. I had no idea how rare these establishments were at the time.) Feeling like the wolves were sufficiently distracted, our cautious yet adventurous heroine makes a beeline for the clerk. No longer bored, he's visibly puzzled by her presence.

"Do you guys have Camp Cuddly Pines Power Tool Massacre?" *she asks. "Because I'd like to buy a copy."*

The clerk takes half a moment to recover from what is apparently the most bizarre question he's ever heard, before he says, "Ehhh, no. We don't sell movies here."

And then, I swear on my skills as a sociologist and an ethnographer, he looked directly in my eyes and said: "You should probably get out of here."

So I left really quickly, throwing up dirt in the parking lot as I sped out of the driveway. I thought I was going to have a heart attack, but I calmed down as I made my way down the road. I was still on a mission.

The next stop was exactly the opposite of the first sticky-stereotype establishment. In fact, if a chain-grocery emporium were to transform into a sex shop, it would've been this store. Imagine a fenced mega parking lot behind a huge modern building gushing light into the Texas night, a security-type person at the door checking IDs before customers were permitted to walk through some sort of metal detector/theft deterrent barrier, and fluorescent bulbs glaring over endless aisles packed with what looked like a billion DVD cases.

I sauntered up to the front door, flashed my ID, and attempted to look casual, while I hid my face from people who weren't paying the slightest bit of attention to me. I began searching for something like a new-release wall, or perhaps a sign with the production studio's name on it . . . you know, like the ones that are suspended from the ceiling in the supermarket for canned vegetables and sports drinks. But a near collision with a young couple on the dildo aisle (this place was full service) and a cheery, fresh-faced young man asking if I needed any help sent me scurrying back into the night.

As I quickly made my way out of the parking lot (no time to linger—the security cameras were on me), I felt like a failure. Apparently I was afraid of porn stores. This might be a problem given my chosen area of study. But hope was not totally lost. There was still one store left on that stretch of road.

From the outside, my third stop looked like an indie video store. On the inside, it looked exactly the same: medium-size, slightly shabby, smelling like sexy oil and patchouli. There was a small turn-stile security gate by the counter at the front door. A friendly, slightly stoned-seeming clerk checked my ID and said to let her (her!) know if I needed anything. I did half a lap before I found the "sports drinks" sign I'd been looking for earlier. Right beneath it, illuminated by rays of light shining down from the porn research gods, was *Camp Cuddly Pines Power Tool Massacre.* I laughed out loud. I almost cried. I picked up the box with two hands and carried it to the counter like a proud child.

"I would like to buy this," I said to the clerk.

"Are you sure?" she asked. "It's a three-disc set, it's kind of expensive. You could just rent it."

"I'm sure," I said.

Minutes later, I did a little skip to my car. My pride was restored; it had only cost $39.95 (plus tax). I still have the receipt.

— x x x —

It's amusing now for me to think about a time in life when I wasn't absolutely steeped in adult content and felt uncomfortable in an adult store. But I was once both. And today, as the years have passed and I'm able to look at porn more critically (read: with a little less emotional spasticity), I wonder how the heck it is that people can make any sense of adult content as a media form and/or a film genre. Even if some-one has seen enough systematically sampled porn to be considered an "expert," sex and gender issues have widely variable meanings. Thus, what's "extreme" or "sexy" or acceptable or whatever is also widely variable. I *really* wonder about this when researchers come to con-clusions about the nature of adult content as a whole based on a few conveniently selected films (which they may or may not have watched themselves) or on a small collection of scenes.

Like any artistic form, erotic films and scenes are two-way mirrors—a sort of cultural looking glass reflecting some dimension of producers' *and* consumers' desires. There is no way to fully capture what porn means to every person who views and/or creates it, but what might adult content say about wider society and culture over time? After my initial foray into *Camp Cuddly Pines Power Tool Massacre*, I decided to delve into that question through rigorous research: I watched twenty-nine systematically sampled key adult films in order to explore patterns and trends occurring in US adult content production and development between 1972 and 2010.[1]

Let me repeat that: I watched *twenty-nine* systematically sampled key adult films, for science.

Right now, you're probably thinking one of two things: *An excuse to watch all that porn—yes!* or *You had to watch all the porn—ugh!* I must confess that I went back and forth between these two extremes myself as I worked my way through this bevy of boobs, butts, and banging. And there were a slew of other emotions that went into it too, including my being completely lost at the outset.

Once I went through a (painstakingly detailed) process in order to figure out exactly which films to watch, the next question was how to make sense of them all. How do you *code* all that content, porn or otherwise? Coding is research-speak for identifying themes, looking for indicators of said themes, and keeping track of how often they happen. In other words, how often do "problematic representations of women" transpire—count, count, count. How often do "instances of body modification" occur—count, count, count. All those themes and indicators times twenty-nine feature-length films. Your head hurts already, doesn't it?

I developed what basically amounted to an elaborate "porn themes spreadsheet" in conjunction with an evolving list of additional (read: unforeseen to my novice eyes at the outset) acts and instances that indicated any one or more of those predetermined ideas and phenomena. Then, armed with a glass of wine and an über-nerdy clipboard, I sat down to code some porn.

At first it was fun. My plan was to watch one film per evening, which basically amounted to a month-long partial reprieve from typing. I decided to skip chronology and, instead, bounce around between eras. That way, I wouldn't get bogged down by any particular decade or aesthetic. I picked out the titles I really wanted to watch first—the ones I was super curious about, the legends, and those shrouded in infamy. Some were amazing; others were disappointing. After about the fifth film, I started to wonder if my neighbors knew what I was doing. And what they were thinking.

Around ten titles in, I switched to beer—it lasted longer—and started talking to the television. "Ugh, don't do that!" I would groan and avert my eyes, or "Move your leg! I can't see." Occasionally, I would just sigh. I had gotten into titles I was unfamiliar with and was beginning to see things that surprised, appalled, and occasionally pleased me. I knew enough industry history at this point to appreciate the cultural significance of some of these films, but mostly I just marveled at how much people could change their language, their hair, and even their bodies over decades, all while still doing the exact same sexual things. And I continued to wonder about my neighbors.

By the time I reached the final five films, I was drinking Red Bull and watching porn at three in the afternoon. I had learned a lot, but I really needed to be done with this. When the last film ended, I did a little dance and ran outside. I had now watched more porn than anyone else in the entire world—or so I thought.

4

Working the Booth

MY FIRST ADULT ENTERTAINMENT EXPO (AEE) WAS IN 2008.

Though it's changed significantly in recent years, AEE is still the most recognizable and prominent adult industry trade show held in the US, therefore probably in the world. All sorts of adult companies and performers come to Las Vegas every January to do business and network with their peers. There are also fan days and areas dedicated to consumers, so various adult entities with some measure of celebrity dedicate time to meeting and greeting the public as well. Honestly, it's not unlike any other professional convention.

But let me tell you, back in 2008, it was *s-h-o-c-k-i-n-g* to me.

You see, I'd heard about AEE from the mainstream media and from other academics—about the raunchiness, the sex everywhere, the sleazy porn dudes peddling clueless chicks, the weirdo fans salivating over girl-meat. It all sounded so . . . pornographic; and I'm not ashamed to admit that the first year I went I was nervous. But that passed rather quickly.

Yes, there was sex everywhere, but it was in the form of film trailers, content advertisements, and marketing displays. There were also booths showcasing sex toys, adventurous bedroom gear, and fetish clothing. But none of this should've been surprising. After all, it was an adult entertainment expo. There was no live, or even simulated, sex happening anywhere, but there were some bits of sexy diversion— pole-dancing demonstrations, fashion shows, ladies handing out penis-shaped lollipops, and fans walking around in various stages of costumed undress. But again, none of this should have been surprising.

Everything I'd ever heard about AEE seemed to be either a gross embellishment or an out-and-out fabrication. The disconnect between what I thought I knew about AEE pre-2008 and the reality of the con-vention itself shocked me more than anything I actually experienced or saw.

And what exactly did I experience or see?

Well, as I was then in the midst of completing fieldwork for my dis-sertation, most of what I did involved helping out in the booth.

Like most other major professional adult production companies, the group I was working with had a booth on the convention floor. It took a lot to run that thing, and in order to get to go to the show, I had to help out. My duties included, but were not limited to: making sure the performers who were signing autographs and meeting fans were comfortable and happy; making sure the fans waiting in ridic-ulously long lines for said performers were somewhat comfortable and happy; making sure businesspeople popping by were appropri-ately directed (or deflected); answering any number of strange and/ or interesting questions; handing out DVD samplers and other swag; carrying boxes; stacking things; finding lip gloss, brushes, cigarettes, mints, tampons, (sugar-free) Red Bull, and innumerable misplaced cell phones. You know, glamorous, sexy stuff.

Occasionally, there were catastrophes.

Like this one time, there was a display of RealDolls[1] in an alcove area of the booth—a little tucked-in side display for fans to ogle as they waited in the autograph line. RealDolls are big and heavy, and each one was suspended in an elaborate display case. We had a gaggle of these giant "Barbie"-like creatures, standing upright in their clear plastic coffins, just beyond a red velvet rope. Disaster was inevitable.

At this particular moment, I was supervising the danger zone: that staging space just before fans get to approach their favorite starlet and the entire queue beyond. I was eagle-eyed at my post, equidistant between the RealDolls and the performers, trying to make sure neither group of ladies was being inappropriately touched or harassed. And though the crowd was thick and the line was long, for a while everything seemed to be going ok.

But then I saw him: a pushy gentleman stepping over the rope barricade, apparently in search of a more intimate photo op. Before I could call out to the nearest security guard—"Watch the girls while I go stop this idiot!"—he had weaseled his way in between the doll on the end and the booth's canvas sidewall. As I pushed past grumbling fans, I saw him lean into her case, struggling to get close. Then she began to sway. The stupidly heavy, upright doll tipped back and forth a couple of times, gathering momentum before bashing into her closest sister.

And then they all started to fall, in slow motion, like giant sex doll dominoes.

Each one made a horrible crashing noise as she hit the concrete floor. One tipped off to the side, smashing into the booth itself and ripping down the sidewall. The entire interior—supplies, boxes and boxes of product, and everyone's personal effects—was exposed to the convention hall, as I stood dumbfounded amid the rubble. The photo-seeking fan scurried off.

It took about an hour for the maintenance folks to gather their wits, pick up the dolls, and repair the damage. In the meantime, I stood at the top of a twelve-foot ladder, creating the illusion of a barricade by holding the canvas up to the booth's metal frame.

When I returned home after that first AEE, I had the worst headache ever.

For several years following that initial experience, AEE didn't really change. At least, it didn't change for me. I would still come home exhausted because I would still do some of the same work—hours and hours spent hunting for lost lip gloss (which was forever MIA) at that very same booth. Because, like any good feminist scholar trained in social justice, I was (and still am) compelled to give back to the community that helped me develop my sociological perspective. Plus, though working in that booth was tiring, it was also pretty dang fun.

I still go to AEE every January. These days, though, I do other things: meet with people who've worked in the business for decades (important!), conduct interviews with all levels and types of performers (also, so important), talk to media, and attend educational seminars and discussions, among many other things. I also began organizing and moderating a Women in Adult speaker series in 2012, in which five to six women from various corners of the industry talk about their workplace experiences and share their insights. So far, each event has been a smashing, meaningful success.

But things are changing for the adult industry, which means they're also changing for AEE. In spite of event planners' best efforts to mask it, the show has decreased in size every year since 2008. There are fewer vendors and fewer fans, and the event is held at a much smaller venue. Most of the swag and all of the lollipops have disappeared. Even my beloved booth is gone. These days, the company simply cordons off a raised stage area for signings. My help is no longer necessary.

The entire adult industry is in great state of flux—and, perhaps because of online piracy and cultural saturation with sex-related media, one might also say in a great state of decline. Many people will tell you that DVD is dead (read: DVDs have stopped selling), and tube sites—sites that steal copyright-protected content and make it available to viewers for free—have essentially convinced consumers that porn is a free commodity rather than a market good.

The issue of piracy on tube sites is extremely complex, but put simply: In porn, a collection of key tube sites have nearly leveled the entire industry. Watching pirated porn has the same effect on performers' and producers' bottom line as watching pirated episodes of *Game of Thrones* or *True Blood*—except that because adult industry folks are working with much smaller budgets and smaller profit margins, each individual visit to a porn tube site has a much more significant impact.

These combined cultural shifts have made it pretty difficult to make money in porn these days. But this decline can't actually be about sex, because sex continues to drive our culture. It's all over the Internet, and we as a society are becoming increasingly sexually aware. So it must really be about adult entertainment. Maybe we've evolved beyond porn-embodied versions of sex and passed the desire to engage our fantasies in person. Maybe we no longer care about meeting our favorite porn stars. Maybe the entire thing has lost its mystery.

It's an interesting question to think about: Has the time and place for porn expired? Are we all just kinda over it?

5

The Thin Line Between
Real and Fake

WHEN I WAS A KID, I WAS A LITTLE KNOW-IT-ALL. I WAS also a ridiculously obsessive planner. I suspect I was rather annoying.

The cataclysmic synergy of these fine qualities came into full bloom during my early undergrad years. I started college "knowing" that I was going to be a doctor (an MD doctor, not a PhD doctor). And not surprisingly, I had my entire course schedule planned the summer before classes began. I even plotted out years' worth of illustrative charts that had been devised in conjunction with a deep and meaningful study of the UCLA general catalogue. At all of seventeen, I knew everything life had in store.

It was around this same time that I got into a mini-debate with a friend of mine. We were discussing something everyone obsessed over during the nineties: breast implants. I was of the mind that breast implants were horrible, atrocious things that corrupted an individual's humanity, as well as the overall integrity of wider society. Basically, bad news. Saul, who was ten years older and ten years wiser and getting his

PhD in aerospace engineering (so, maybe he wasn't that much wiser after all), destroyed my argument with two simple questions.

"Didn't you have braces?" he asked.

"Yes," I responded. What the hell did that have to do with anything?

"Well, isn't that the exact same thing?"

"No!" I asserted immediately and went on making whatever silly argument I was attempting to espouse. But Saul was right: Braces on your teeth and augmentations for your boobs are pretty much the same thing. Both are after-market alterations, they're just perceived differently by a society that holds different parts of gendered human bodies to different standards.

Late-adolescent me would never in a million years acknowledge that Saul had a point, but he did. And it's affected my thinking ever since.

—— x x x ——

Like braces and breast implants, porn is not real. At least, porn is not real in the sense that it's a literal reflection of reality.

Like any other media—a Hollywood film, a bestselling book, or a story on the evening news—porn is crafted. A concept, maybe a script, a director and a crew, lights and makeup, performers, and post-production processing (among many other things) are all required to create fantasy visions of various sexual encounters. Sometimes porn may attempt to recreate an actual social or historical happening, and sometimes porn may take inspiration from existing cultural artifacts, but, in the end, it's all just smoke and mirrors and a version of a story.

But, though porn is not real, its creation most certainly involves real people. Real people make porn. Porn performers are real humans who engage in some form of physical sexual performance with other real humans, and they all agree to work with one another long before the cameras start rolling. At least, in professional adult content production they do. Consequently, some level of chemistry, even if it's in the form of chagrined resignation, between work-partnered performers must also exist.

Despite this, people greatly enjoy debating the authenticity of sex in porn. I sometimes find this funny because what exactly is there to debate? Real live people are doing it, so clearly the action—the literal sex—is real. Somewhere, at some time during production, porn sex actually happened. But porn sex is also contrived, happening in positions and lasting for durations of time that would be nearly impossible for nonprofessionals to achieve. The scenarios don't exist, and taboos are flouted that probably shouldn't be. (In real life, I mean; imagination is imagination.)

These maneuverings and manipulations complicate things, and, regardless of what one thinks the effect may be, it's safe to say that most people feel porn may have some impact on real-life sex. *May* have some impact? Fine, I can get behind that idea. But what confounds me is the notion that porn *must* have an impact and that the impact must be a significant one. By that logic, all texts in all media forms *must* have a significant impact on consumers. For example, *The Fast and The Furious* series of films then also *must* have a significant impact on consumers' driving. But no one would ever argue that. I think this notion that porn *must* impact you is tied into our cultural tendencies and mental blocks related to sex, sex education, and—ultimately—judgment and shame. But that's a whole other topic.

Getting back to real and fake, what we're ultimately left with are two aspects of porn—the production that actually happens in real life and the final finished product that consumers get to see. Most times, these are two very different realities. In the case of a Hollywood movie—think of spy flicks, horror films, and car-chase scenes—we're pretty aware of the distinction; we understand it. In the world of porn though? Not so much.

The conflation of pornographic reality and fantasy has manifested in all sorts of interesting and problematic ways, from consumers using adult content as a sexual teaching tool to people gauging their self-worth against the images they see in the newest adult scenarios. But it's not just consumers who are caught up in the tension between real and fake. Producers and performers must also navigate these choppy waters and changing tides, while trying to determine how far they want to take their claims of authenticity. When we're talking about porn, what constitutes real and what counts as fake? How do these dimensions emerge in content? What specific markers are used to gauge what's real (and fake), and how do they vary? This is something I've been thinking about for a while now. To me, it seems that, in contemporary porn, a lot of related attention swirls around the two Bs: boobs and bush.

For the sake of discussion, let's look at producers Elegant Angel. In adult content's entire collective past and present, nothing compares to this studio's offerings. Elegant Angel puts out a wealth of sexy-luscious, highly stylized series, as well as an occasional feature film. And though some of the titles may seem off-putting (for example, *Big Wet Asses* and *Massive Facials* are two of their more popular series), don't be fooled. If harder content coupled with a very refined aesthetic is your thing, you need look no further. But this studio and its skilled directors are not immune to the trends of boobs and bush and real and fake currently influencing adult content. Consider their one-off title *Natural* and their series *Bush*, both of which came about in 2011.

There are five scenes in *Natural*, all fairly straightforward and all epitomizing Elegant Angel's unique, starkly beautiful aesthetic. And all, allegedly, "natural."

I struggle with this attribution—natural. It's extremely widespread, but what does it mean? In the contemporary porn lexicon "natural" is simply code for "no boob jobs," but I just can't get over the fact that the lack of boob jobs is the *only* natural thing about the women performers in this film. From the settings, the lighting, and the oil and water being misted or poured over various body parts, to the fact that most of the women performers have tattoos, all of them have beautiful hair and makeup, and one has had fairly significant cosmetic dental work, everything is contrived. These things are all well and good, but they're not natural.

And why does natural just mean no boob jobs? Why stop there? Why not rule out altered noses or lips, artificial nails, or tattoos? It really makes very little sense. For example, no one would ever call the currently untattooed Kagney Linn Karter (who is featured in *Natural*'s bonus scene) natural, but her implants probably took less time to complete than Hayden Winters' elaborate ink (Hayden is featured in the actual film), and Kagney wears no more or less makeup than any of her contemporaries. Neither Kagney nor Hayden is unaltered; and when you really think about it, no one is. So I struggle with referring to anything in the modern world as natural, especially in film projects and even more so in porn.

Less invasive but equally confounding are trends associated with pubic topiary, or the manicuring of bush.

Our world is filled with fads. What's hot one day will soon be not and will likely cycle back around again. It's a sociocultural thing that happens with music, food, fashion, politics . . . and pubic hair. Pubic hair has been styled for various reasons for hundreds of years, and we've gone through many looks. From the wearing of merkins (pubic wigs that were historically used following shaving to combat lice and are now used for fun and as costuming in performance art) to the voluminous seventies' bush, these hair-down-there styles are just as faddish as anything else.

In contemporary porn, although hairy has long been (and continues to be) a significant niche, the vast majority of performers tend to be *relatively* hairless. (Well, at least they are when they're on camera.) Trends range from all to mostly bare in the most visible content, and even the women and films touting bush present very specifically manicured configurations.

Though it's impossible to determine if performers dictate the styles that show up in content or if consumers demand specific looks, to which performers and producers respond (I think it's both and more), these pubic hair patterns provide a wealth of fodder for debates about the wider social implications of such manicuring in general.

At one end of the spectrum, there's an increasingly vocal contingent that feels a woman's pubic hair is hers to style and/or remove as she sees fit. At the other are those who maintain certain forms of pubic topiary are unnatural and have substantial negative social implications. And in between are folks who hold just about every other opinion about every other configuration of pubes imaginable.

Lately though, some people have been talking about the bush in a new way. Supposedly, it's back! And in some respects, based on my observations, it is. But not like you'd think. The mainstream adult industry's current love affair with hair does not involve seventies-era nostalgia or any semblance of natural. Actually, it's just another trending coif.

Consider Elegant Angel's series *Bush*. It consists of well-done titles that showcase the latest craze in pubic topiary—long on top and bare on the sides and around back. This look always makes me think of nineties-era *Beverly Hills, 90210* and its character David Silver. He sported the same look, just on his head—long on top and shaved on the sides and around back. What we're seeing now is simply a David Silver for the *mons veneris*. This configuration satisfies many needs in contemporary porn, namely, getting a good penetration shot, while still attempting to embody an air of unwaxed, unshaven realness. But just as Hayden Winters' "natural" tattoos ring false, these bits of David Silver–styled bush feel more like marketing than authenticity.

Films like these do not mean the bush is back. Instead, they're simply evidence of an emerging style. Will this configuration become the landing strip of today? Will the rest of the world soon be blaming porn for the long-on-top, shaved-on-the-sides-and-around-back look? And most importantly, what cutesy name will bikini waxers and estheticians come up with for this request? Perhaps the David Silver!

I kid. But seriously—whether we're talking about boobs or bush or braces or sex or music or food (or anything else), consistency and authenticity in contemporary media is a tricky subject full of pitfalls. I sometimes wish that, rather than trying to convince themselves something is real or fake, people would simply experience the creation, whatever it is.

But maybe that's just me.

6

Average Joes and the Monster Cock

I ONCE RAN INTO THE LEGENDARY AND LAUDED ADULT performer Rod Johnson in the lobby of Sexytime Products. Sexytime is a leading manufacturer of adult novelties—porno speak for sex toys. I was super excited to see Rod, as we are buddies in real life and it had been a while, so we spent a few minutes chatting before it even occurred to me to ask him what the heck he was doing there.

It seems that Rod was there that day to pick up his penis, two of them actually. Apparently, Sexytime had recently molded and manufactured a sex toy version of Rod's cock, and the company was in the process of distributing it across the land! As he and I were standing there talking, someone from the warehouse brought out two fancy boxes, units of product ready to go. Rod continued to chat, never missing a beat, but I was distracted. I immediately grabbed the closest box, eager to get a better look. I had seen plenty of his work, but I'd never actually studied the goods up close before. How did his penis stack up?

The packaging was impressive, the size of a large shoebox, with a clear plastic window on the front. One could easily peer in, gazing upon the impressive prize suspended inside its packaging shell. The box's remaining sides were glossy and colorful, covered with smoldering, seductive images of Rod's bad-boy face. And there was list of the unit's advantages and features. These included being modeled after Rod's real-life cock, as well as boasting that the contents constituted a realistic, seven-inch ("actual size"), insertable, waterproof, harness compatible, phthalate-free novelty. Each unit came complete with a hand-painted pink tip and "true-to-life saggy balls."

True-to-life saggy balls.

"Why do you need two . . . er, three . . . of these?" I asked.

His response was not nearly as titillating as I would have liked. Apparently, Rod was traveling over the next week with his girlfriend, Phoenix Lee. Phoenix had several feature dance bookings and radio show appearances lined up, and one program director had set up a contest for listeners. Winners would receive one of Phoenix's sex toys, a molded and manufactured replica of her external genitalia. The station had asked Rod to bring his toy in as a gag prize for the losers. Rod took this request with a grain of salt, but the whole thing seemed rather unkind to me.

We parted ways soon after, and, honestly, I didn't think much more about it. It's not so uncommon for performers of Rod's caliber to have their own novelty dildo dong thing, and I've long since given up trying to figure out why anyone would want two penises instead of one . . . or none . . . or three . . . or otherwise.

I found myself thinking about Rod's rod sometime later though, after a PR announcement of epically ordinary proportions found its way into my inbox. Apparently Topco Sales, another leading adult novelty manufacturer, had just launched its Average Joe line of realistic dongs. Relative to Rod's toy, these novelty items were rendered in more "average" sizes, because, as their marketing materials suggested, "not everyone wants to play with a porn-sized cock."

The Average Joe line consisted of six different dongs. Each Average Joe was realistic, waterproof, phthalate free, and harness compatible, just like Rod's replica. But unlike Rod's toy, none of the Average Joes were claiming to reflect an actual person. Instead, each Average Joe had an invented name and some sort of fantasy identity attached to it. Victor the Construction Worker, Darnell the Fitness Instructor, and three other Joes each measured in at an impressively average six inches, while one guy, Andy the Mechanic, was an extra-usual 5.5 inches.

What I found especially interesting about these Average Joes was that, in spite of their complete and total fakeness, each was allegedly bringing a different sort of "realness" to the table. Supposedly, they were more representative of an average person's reality than Rod's porn-size cock. But that didn't make sense to me. Rod was real, as was his penis. How could an Average Joe be more real than Rod? I found it interesting that the contrived realness of the Average Joes was being presented as somehow better or more authentic than an exact replication of Rod's rod.

Then I started thinking about Rod himself. For him, maybe those Average Joes didn't even register. Perhaps he didn't even think about the fact that if they were truly "average" then he was outside the norm (above the curve or otherwise). And for Rod, because those boxes containing molds of his own cock were actual embodiments of what he had and who he was, maybe he never once considered that the Average Joes (who were pure fiction) were being marketed as more "real" than he—an actual real human—was. But I thought about all of this. And what about other penis-wielding sorts? What might they think about Rod and all those Average Joes? Because if the mystique of women porn performers' bodily proportions, including overall physique, breast size, apparent genitalia, and more, can induce insecurities in ladies (as is so often claimed), what might all seven inches of Rod's rod do to others with variably sized rods themselves? It was interesting to consider the novelty dildo and the balance between porn star penises, Average Joes, and the ever-elusive Monster Cock.

There are a wide range of dongs available in the adult novelty world. Rod's toy and the Average Joes are nowhere near the only ones, as a quick search of "dildo sex toys" at any conventional sex toy website reveals. For example, at some point, I searched through the well-known, well-developed, and (according to Alexa.com) well-trafficked AdamEve.com. At the time, I found everything from the 5.5-inch-long, 1-inch-thick, pretty pink Femme Rubber Dildo to the 11-inch-long, 2-inch-thick Double Bullet Jumbo Dildo. There was also the 8.5-inch-long Carmen's Fun Cock: EXTRA LARGE (1.5 inches thick, FYI) and the 15-inch-long, 2-inch-thick King Dong Dildo—the "biggest dildo ever!" Now granted, the King Dong Dildo is cross-marketed as a joke gift, a for-fun novelty if you will. But you only have to look a little further into more advanced corners of the sex toy world to find the WildFire Extra-Large SensaFirm Black-Balled Cock (11 inches long, 3 inches thick)—a toy made for actual use that comes with a safety disclaimer.

The real-world approximate average erect length for a human penis is five to six inches. But in the world of novelty cocks, real-world average falls on the small end of the spectrum—the pretty pink beginner end. And leading porn performers aren't really packin' that much more. Yes, Rod is longer than average, but he is nowhere near 11 inches. This implies that, relative to the sex toy world, average (and Average Joe) penises and porn-size cocks are actually small. Anything progressively larger is for a more advanced user.

People often talk about the disconnects between women and sex in porn and real women and real sex in real life, highlighting the presumably negative effects these disconnects have on the wider social world. I find this type of rhetoric to be somewhat shortsighted and tedious, if for no other reason than the people in porn are themselves completely real, as is the sex that they're having. And you can't generalize about the impact a series of images or fantasy presentations are going to have on people. What may stir fear or revulsion in one person may be the hottest thing ever to the next; what may make one person insecure may be inspiring to another.

But I do wonder about the impact sex toy marketing might have on men. Not that I think it has any single uniform consequence, but clearly fantasy is different from reality when it comes to penis prosthetics. If one is concerned with the effects of adult imagery on women, why not also worry about the effects a girl-girl scene featuring a Foot Long Double Dildo (1.5 inches thick) may have on an actual average Joe named Andy, mechanic or otherwise?

7

On Set

THE FIRST TIME I WAS ON A PORN SET—DURING ACTUAL
shooting, I mean—it was a big deal, but not because anything outlandish or unexpected happened. It was a big deal because I had
never experienced such a thing before. I was nervous, I was sweat-
ing, and I was afraid I would make the performers uncomfortable or
knock something over. Plus, let's be honest here—I'd seen all those
black-light scenes in crime shows, and I was worried about . . . dried
substances.

My first time on set was also a big deal because, while I was relatively keyed up, everyone else seemed absolutely absorbed with (or
totally bored by) their jobs. The fact that doing said jobs involved
recording two people having sex didn't seem to matter much at all.

I was flabbergasted.

But after about ten minutes or so of a director working with some
naked guy who took instructions and made adjustments to his cock's
position near an equally naked woman who was on all fours at the foot
of some prop futon, I started to calm down. Outside of the attention
it took to get the job done, no one cared. No one was weirded out,

except me, and there was nothing going on besides work. I was eventually able to refocus my attention on the labor of the situation.

But then the performers changed positions, and I had to start the work-normalization process all over again. Such was the required learning curve, I guess.

Since then, I've been on numerous sets, while numerous types of sex were being filmed for various types of porn. It's become far less stressful. One time, on one set, I actually dozed off.

I had been invited to the set of *American Dad XXX*—a satirical take on Fox's animated *American Dad!* sitcom. Parodies were so hot around 2010 that anything was fair game. Even cartoons. There's a *Simpsons* porn parody and one of *South Park*—no joke.

Getting an invite to the *American Dad XXX* set wasn't really a big deal. I received such invitations regularly, but not because I was special or anything. Though these events were never open to the public, industry reporters, bloggers, and folks who were trying to show the adult industry and adult content production in a more complex light often were invited. The hope was for media coverage, which was all part of building some pre-release buzz.

This is what the invitation said:

Exquisite Films and Paradox Pictures invite media to attend the set of *American Dad XXX* on [Date X]. This real-life rendition of the popular animated series features a star-studded cast. . . . [Date X] will mark the first day of production on *American Dad XXX* and [will] include sex scenes, dialogue scenes, glamour photos, and box cover photos. . . .

Decisions, decisions. Though I had never once watched an episode of *American Dad!*, I hadn't been on set in a while. I had to be in the

Valley that day anyway, and a friend of mine whom I hadn't seen for some time had to be there, too. We'd be able to catch up over lunch afterward, so I decided to pop in.

I got to the set just after 11 a.m. Everything was set up inside one of about six or so storefronts making up an innocuous, commercial/industrial building in the middle of a nondescript mixed-use block—residential on one side of the street, commercial on the other. There was nothing about the location's exterior that suggested porn was being shot inside.

And truthfully, when you first entered the building, you wouldn't have known it either. Two nice ladies greeted me, and a representative from the company's PR management team introduced me to other media and visitors in attendance. While waiting in the little break/snack/lounging room, I got the pleasant surprise of meeting and chatting with Kim Airs, the proprietrix of Grand Opening, a "sexuality boutique" (her description). In addition to running Grand Opening, Kim is a sex toy consultant who reviews adult novelties, lectures on college campuses, and offers advice to doctors and patients dealing with sex-related problems caused by medical issues. I had known about Kim for a while and was super excited to meet her in person.

We engaged in some gushing mutual love of each other's work and eventually moseyed onto the actual set. There were four rooms built out in a larger warehouse, each designed to look something like *American Dad!*—a conventional home, except really brightly colored. Kim and I continued our chat while photographers snapped away at sex bomb Angelina Valentine and, eventually, Evan Stone. They were booked to work together in the first scene of the day. We found some folding chairs and pulled up a seat.

And then it was hurry up and wait as everyone seemed to get ready for, well, I'm not sure what. A couple of informal interviews were going on around the room, Angelina and Evan were practicing their lines, production assistants were scampering around doing all sorts of preparation-looking things. Kim got some texts that she had to attend to and stepped outside. I started to get a little sleepy, so I ate a banana and drank some water.

A photographer had started shooting Angelina, who was in the most awkward-looking position: one leg up and across a dining room table, looking over the opposite shoulder, while balanced on the tallest platform shoe ever. She made it seem effortless. Evan was now off to the side, joking with some reporter, and I could hear him laughing. It was kinda warm in there, and my head was starting to nod to one side. The lights were strangely bright. Then it got hot . . . then dim.

And then suddenly everything was very bright and glamorous and incredible. Glitter started to fall from the ceiling, covering the floor with a light dusting of silver sparkle. Pink neon ran along every line and corner in the room—I was in a sparkly pink spider web. Evan walked up to me. Inexplicably, he was wearing an orange and pink ringmaster's costume and carrying an ornate platter. I was eyeing the trio of baby goats walking alongside him (where did they come from?) when he leaned over and offered me some pizza and a glass of champagne. Wait! Where was I? Where was Kim? Did I just doze off in my chair?

Not quite—I didn't actually fall asleep, but I *was* in that in-between dreaming state. That's how anti-climactic everything was. And I was starting to get *really* hungry after all that waiting. Consequently, when everyone finally seemed ready to start the scene, I had a big decision to make: Because you can't go walking on and off set all willy-nilly while people are shooting (due to noise and whatnot), I had to decide if I wanted to leave for lunch now or in about an hour.

My pal, who had just arrived, opted for the former. We ducked out and proceeded to check out this nifty South African spot around the corner. I had some delicious black bean soup and three samosas.

But things on a porn set aren't always that ordinary. Sometimes, a set can reveal all sorts of gaps in the space-time continuum—breaches in reality that trouble the "normal" order of things. People move through various stages of intimacy in ways that may seem counterintuitive to individuals in the outside world, people embrace environmental factors that would never be acceptable during ordinary exchanges, and jokes that would usually get a guy slapped become acceptable, even hilarious.

For example, I once met with a big-deal Internet content producer about a survey-based research project I was trying to get going. Ever the innovator, Walter Wright was in the midst of populating his newest venture, HorizontalGloryHoles.com. Walter was somewhat atypical in the level of involvement he had during the pre-launch phases of his projects, which was probably a key to his success. Because of his schedule and mine, we ended up having to meet on set. Ordinarily it would be strange to have a research/business meeting on a film set, but in porn this is no big deal.

I pulled up to a gorgeous residential home in the west San Fernando Valley a perfect ten minutes early. I adjusted my too-short-for-everyday businessy dress, slipped on my shoes (I'm not good at driving in heels), and texted Walter. They weren't supposed to be shooting yet, but I didn't want to risk charging in mid-scene.

Before I even made it to the door though, it was flung open by my friend Scott. Scott was a one-time performer-turned-production-manager who happened to be on set that day. What a surprise! As we were kissing our hellos and hustling inside, Scott let me know that our buddy Ted was the day's director. Two friends—a double surprise! I edged my way around the alcove, trying not to crush the miniature

Pomeranian dancing at my feet, while also getting the lay of the land. The set appeared to be in the living room: a massage table surrounded by lights and a static camera. I said a quick hello to Ted, who was a little frantic, and greeted a man and a woman—the performers—whom I didn't know. Then Walter appeared and shuttled me past the set, down a long hallway, and into the home office.

After an hour's worth of very productive conversation behind closed doors, the small room was starting to get a little warm. The air conditioner had to be off, as even the tiniest bit of ambient noise would interrupt the scene. But what was going on out there anyway? We'd been gone for a long time. Perhaps it was supposed to be a lengthy massage? Walter got up to listen near the door.

"Don't make any noise!" I whispered with mock shushing. "You'll mess up the scene, and Ted will kill you!"

"Yeah, plus the money guy will get pissed," he said with a wink.

After a long, quiet thirty seconds, Walter inched the door open. Scott, who was standing behind the static camera, spied him from down the hall and called out, "You guys can come out. We're just waiting for him to pop."

I tailed Walter down the hall and crept into the main room where Scott was. The woman and man I'd seen earlier were going at it through a—wait for it—horizontal glory hole! The man was face down on top of the massage table with his penis pushed through an opening, while the woman was beneath, sucking and popping and jerking. Ted was down there too, on his back and right in the mix, getting it all from another angle with a second camera.

As I tiptoed by, just a few feet away, I got an eyeful of the guy's ass. He was shiny with sweat and had huge tense indentations on either butt check. Apparently the horizontal glory hole was working. And since Scott said I didn't have to be quiet, I whispered loudly "Bye, Ted!"

Without moving the camera even one millimeter, Ted rolled his eyes sideways to look over at me. "Nice to see you for ten seconds. Glad I got to look up your dress," he said.

Ted was nowhere near to looking up my dress, but he probably needed to imagine himself away from the underside of another man's testicles for a moment. Or he needed to imagine his lower back out of the extremely uncomfortable-looking position it was in. Either way, I laughed as I made my way outside. The performers never missed a beat.

It was just another meeting in Porn Valley.

8

Academic Snubbery

A SOCIOLOGIST'S RESEARCH IS NEVER DONE.

Sociologists explore, observe, and try to make sense out of human behavior. Sounds simple enough, except that it's anything but.

Humans are dynamic creatures who are always doing something, and sometimes that something is something new and exciting. But trying to formulate conclusions about social phenomena that are always changing can get complicated, and weighty issues often arise. Issues such as:

1. If you're observing a group or interviewing people about their lived experiences, when is it time to stop? When do you have enough information? Grounded Theory, a methodological approach frequently used in the social sciences, says it's when you start to see repetition, but feminist scholarship and social justice tell us that every experience is significant. How, then, do you split the difference? How do you balance and prioritize observable patterns, avoiding repetition, and an infinite number of data points—points that each essentially amount to an individual's perspective?

2. And what about things that are changing overall, both on an individual and a societal level? Because humans are constantly changing, society is constantly changing. Inversely, since society is constantly changing, humans are also constantly changing. How, then, do you account for overall evolutions, both as a society and on the level of the individual, while observing subcultural patterns and processes?

3. Further, because new things are always coming up, how do you keep the happenings you're describing and addressing from being incomplete and possibly dated? This is made worse by the fact that academic publishing takes so, so (so) long! For example, one article of mine (in the journal *Gender, Work & Organization*) took *twenty-six months* to peer-review and revise. Trust me, this wasn't because I was slacking. Those twenty-six months (a) Were in addition to the years it took me to research and write the piece in the first place, and (b) Do not include the additional time it took for the journal to get the article in an actual volume. My work "early-released" online in 2011, but it wasn't officially published until 2013. Let me state this in another way: Research I conducted in 2007 was finally published in 2013. When you think about these sorts of timelines, it's no wonder people talk about the irrelevance and disconnected inefficacy plaguing academia. But that's the way the system is. When dealing with the slow-moving scholarship leviathan on one hand and the instant gratification that rules contemporary culture on the other, how does an up-and-coming scholar trying to get by avoid losing any understanding of or connection with the people they've observed?

4. And finally, isn't this whole process kind of exploitative and elitist? Entering a community; getting into its business and space; expecting honesty, authenticity, and disclosure; and then running back to the safety of the ivory tower? That get- in/get-out scenario, which is fairly typical of all types of social research, never seemed very social-justicey or feminist-centered to me.

So I've never done that.

I've stayed connected to the adult industry over the years. I give back to the community by volunteering my time and developing expertise. I stay abreast of industry happenings and their wider social relevance, which has allowed me to comment in mainstream media and cultural outlets when occasions arise. And I try to direct critical and multi-faceted academic attention toward the adult community through my developing work.

This doesn't always go over well, though.

One especially brutal moment happened at the American Sociological Association's annual meeting a few years ago.

Just about every line of work or occupation has a professional organization associated with it—physicians have the American Medical Association (AMA), teachers and educators have the Association of American Educators (AAE), and sociologists have the American Sociological Association (ASA). Generally speaking, these national nonprofits are dedicated to advancing the mission, goals, and community associated with their respective discipline or vocation. Not too wild a concept at all.

The ASA has been around for more than one hundred years and has thousands of members—according to its website, more than fourteen thousand in 2012. Members consist of college and university faculty, researchers, students, and people working in government, as well as in the private sector. The organization publishes numerous well-respected scholarly journals (a couple of which are considered career-slam-dunk-caliber folios) intended to further the notion that sociology is a scientific discipline and a profession committed to serving the public good. The ASA also hosts an annual late-summer meeting, and "going to ASA" is one of those things that everyone just seems to do. The whole scene is as much about being seen as it is about sharing ideas, and I have attended multiple times.

The event itself is always huge, spanning about four days, with a few keynote and plenary presentations occurring throughout. These events, which are always delivered by members of the sociological elite, highlight big-deal research, presidential musings, and the overall state of society. Most folks, however, are not elite, and the overwhelming majority of sociologists present their work on three-to-five-person panels or during round-table discussions. There are literally hundreds of panels and round-tables taking place over the course of the event, and they're often just as anticlimactic as they sound. Which then means that attending the bigger and presumably more exciting events, hobnobbing at evening mixers, and sighting celebrity sociologists in the elevators are all must-dos.

Going to ASA isn't cheap. You pay for travel (meetings are held in a different major city every year), a hefty registration fee, and room and board—all this on top of the organization's yearly membership fee. This is a big sum for graduate students especially, who are often living below the poverty line. You could stay off-site at a hostel or with a friend (or friend of a friend of a friend . . .) to save money, but rubbing elbows at the conference hotel is too essential an opportunity to pass up. Consequently, students often bunk four-or-more-to-a-room at whatever Hyatt or Marriott is hosting ASA that year. It's through these sorts of arrangements that I've ended up sleeping with (read: sharing a bed surface with) more than one total stranger and showering while various folks use the vanity. Nothing even remotely like either of these scenarios has ever happened to me via porn, but such is the sexy and scintillating life of a budding academic.

Anyway, my department at UT was offering graduate students with accepted papers a generous $500 to help defray the cost of ASA that year.[1] So I did what was informally required of me and traveled to the city of the year for about thirty-six hours. My talk was scheduled for the second-to-last time slot on the final day of the conference, at the tail-end of everything. And because I couldn't afford to arrive earlier, I missed all the key hobnobbing.

I arrived the day before my presentation and tooled around the city. That night, I slept on a hotel-room floor while a mix of friends and strangers slept in the beds. (I was a late addition.) I did everything I could to keep my one pair of nice pants wrinkle free, tried not to spend too much money, and almost broke even. And I was actually excited to present my work. I had put together a preliminary write-up of the key adult film data I had gathered as part of my dissertation, and this ASA was to be its debut.

I was also excited about the other three people I would be presenting with. Though nobody's work was similar to mine, their papers were about various aspects of media representation, and I have always loved media representation. If that weren't enough, two of the other authors were fresh out of graduate school, so not too far removed from me in terms of career development, and the other was a gender sociology legend! I had studied some of Dr. Gender Sociology Legend's work during my master's research, and my CSUN mentor had even given me a copy of one of her key works as a gift years earlier. With all that history, I was excited.

Silly me.

I showed up at the presentation area well in advance; but, after a few minutes, something seemed to be amiss. Besides me, there were a couple of people waiting to hear the talks, and the person who organized the group was there too, but no one else. No other speakers. At all.

At exactly one minute before we were scheduled to begin, Dr. Gender Sociology Legend breezed into the room and took a seat in the presenters' area. She had no notes with her, just a bottle of water and her ASA badge. I thought she was a superhero—so experienced and poised, she didn't even need the obsessive stack of papers and a power-point presentation like I did. Starstruck, I was about to introduce myself when the organizer sidled up.

"Ummm . . . hello, Dr. Legend. I'm The Organizer. We're just going to wait a couple more minutes. We seem to be missing some panelists."

Dr. Gender Sociology Legend looked understandably annoyed. I tried to look annoyed, too. But what could I say? Did I go for the patient and understanding, "Gee, I hope the others are okay." Or should I opt for the more exasperated, "How unprofessional, sheesh!"

Three to four painfully slow minutes ticked by. I had decided on a hybrid approach: "Certainly the other panelists wouldn't dream of being this inconsiderate without good cause. . . ," when Dr. Legend rustled her way to standing. The Organizer jumped in:

"Why don't we go ahead and get started?" she suggested brightly.

"With just me?"

"No, no, of course not. Chauntelle is here, too."

Dr. Gender Sociology Legend finally noticed me. "Which paper are you presenting?" she asked.

I finally managed to find my voice: "The one about the gendered content of adult films. We could just present our papers. Maybe they'll still show up, but if not we'll have plenty of time for a nice discus—"

"Are you talking about pornography?" she cut me off. And then, without waiting for me to stammer a reply, added, "No. I don't think so."

She picked up her water and walked out of the room without another word. I was dumbfounded and embarrassed. The Organizer had to scrape her jaw off the floor and pop her eyes back into her head. The handful of other people present looked uncomfortable and a bit bewildered.

Long moments passed. The Organizer was still at a loss for words. And even though I was blushing hard and felt like a total fool, I smiled and said something along the lines of: "Well, I guess I'll go first then."

This memory still pisses me off. And it still feels just as humiliating. Obviously, I had no problem speaking in front of people, and I wasn't at all nervous about the quality of my scholarship, but I was upset about what I perceived to be a slight that had everything to do with the nature of my work. *Are you talking about pornography?* Sure, it could've been that Dr. Gender Sociology Legend was just over ASA. This encounter occurred during the final few hours of the conference. But she had agreed to speak, and something about her brusque walkout didn't suggest she was tired.

After a talk that I really don't remember and some questions that didn't really matter, I stalked out of the stupid conference hotel, dragging my stupid backpack and stupid laptop over to the stupid metro station. I was no longer concerned with maintaining a professional appearance or avoiding wrinkles. To add insult to injury, I had booked a fairly late flight—you know, thinking I might have the opportunity to caucus with people about big sociological ideas or fantastic new projects after my brilliant presentation. Instead, I got to the airport with hours to spare. And as I sat in a remote corner, licking my wounds with only some pricey airport Internet to keep me company, I stared out the window and wondered, not for the first time (and definitely not for the last), what the hell was I doing playing this academia game.

When I finally made it home, it was well past midnight, but I immediately pulled Dr. Gender Sociology Legend's book off my shelf. After so many years and a move halfway across the country, I still had it. I carefully tore out the page where my CSUN mentor had written me a little note, which I stowed lovingly in a folder. Then I walked that legendary book out to my apartment complex's community dumpster. It was a hot, nasty August night in Central Texas, and the smell was horrifically ripe. I thought Dr. Gender Sociology Legend's book would be happy at home with the rest of the garbage.

I watched it sail into the bin and reveled in the wet slap-squish noise that marked its touchdown. Maybe it was petty of me, but oh well.

9

The Slippery Slope of Subjectivity

I WATCH A LOT OF PORN.

It's important for the work I do. You can't really understand an industry if you're not fully versed in its products. Plus there's an interactive relationship between the adult community and wider society such that each impacts and influences the other. Within this context, bits of adult content act like snapshots, and these captured moments reflect various dimensions of porn and society's ever-evolving relationship with it. It's interesting to think about: Things like porn parodies and star showcases act as evidence that the two worlds do, in fact, interrelate.

So I watch a lot of porn. But just because I watch a lot of porn doesn't mean I like everything I see. In fact, I'm kind of a tough critic.

I try to look at adult content as a whole, both as a unique project and within the context of all porn, all media, and the collective social world. And because I'm so familiar with so much porn (as well as popular culture and wider society), I'm often able to make connections that others may not. I sometimes try to consider relatively "objective" dimensions of the medium, such as production values; but, anyone who knows something about objectivity knows that what's considered objective is as biased as anything. Everything we create, write, or think is filtered through a subjective human experience, thus everything is embedded with at least a little bit of bias. Thus, because I'm me and I think all the things that I do, my perspectives and biases influence my views. My assessments of adult content are mostly—okay, entirely—subjective. They're informed by my mind, my history, and my work.

It doesn't happen often, but sometimes my personal views get in the way. I once got a great lesson about slippery slopes and my own subjective assessments through reviews I wrote for two films: Burning Angel Entertainment's *Joanna Angel: Ass-Fucked* and Extreme Comixxx's *The Justice League of Pornstar Heroes*.

But before I get to my reviews, it's important to have a bit of background on the companies behind those films. Burning Angel is an alt-type adult production company that specializes in a sort of punk/emo/tattooed sexy-campy aesthetic and lifestyle. It was founded by Rutgers alum Joanna Angel, who produces, directs, and stars in a lot of Burning Angel content and generally masterminds everything else related to her porno mini-empire. She's pretty impressive.

Burning Angel creates web-based content and all-sex DVD collections, as well as funny movies—tongue-in-cheek titles like *Kung Fu Pussy* and the *Footloose* knock-off *Asphyxia Heels The World*. Sometimes Burning Angel titles are sublimely clever slam-dunks, like *Doppelgänger*. Other times, the company makes huge missteps, like its use of yellowface (which is akin to blackface) in *The Walking Dead: A Hardcore Parody*. But no one and nothing is perfect all of the time—such is the variability of human experience.

Ass-Fucked is one example of porn at its finest: five anal trysts, all featuring various iterations of Joanna, that I absolutely loved. The scenes range from cutesy and fun, like the one where two Jewish youngsters (Joanna and James Deen) are celebrating Christmas, to intense and hyper-hot, like the final scene in the collection, the one where Joanna has way too much anal sex with Manuel Ferrara. This scene was especially impressive—a breathless, exhilarating conclusion.

In terms of hot porno, *Ass-Fucked* delivered in spades. But in my view, this film wasn't so much erotic as it was empowering. It showed an educated woman business owner in control of exactly the kind of sex she wanted, all in order to make exactly the kind of creative product she wanted to sell. And the fact that, at moments, the film was a bit too intense for my personal tastes made it that much better. I didn't have to like everything about *Ass-Fucked* to appreciate how powerful it was. It was one of those projects that should be cited when people claim women adult performers do not enjoy their work. Sometimes, some of them clearly, obviously, totally do.

But soon after I got rocked by *Ass-Fucked*, I watched *The Justice League of Pornstar Heroes*. What a cold, gross letdown.

This is what it's about:

> When a great evil threatens porn's very existence, The Justice League of Porn Star Heroes comes together to battle the Legion of Poon. Can Batman and Robin tag-team Catwoman into submission? Are Wonder Woman's truth juices enough to get the General talking? Will the sexy Mob Boss stop The Flash in his tracks? Can Superman get Zatanna to turn a real trick? Will the Green Lantern let Harley Quinn strip him of his ring and more? What are Lex Luthor and Poison Ivy scheming? Can our porn star heroes save the day? Only watching *The Justice League XXX* will reveal the answers, as the porn star heroes try to save the world, one orgy at a time.

What's not mentioned in this synopsis is that the director of *The Justice League* is one of the most notorious bad apples in the porn business. He's disrespectful to performers, bounces checks, and is generally difficult to work with. I knew this going into my viewing, and I evaluated the film accordingly.

The content itself was good—high production value and a decently plausible super-storyline. There were seven total sex scenes interwoven throughout the narrative, all ranging from fine to good, except for the final blowbang scene. For those of you who may not know, a blowbang is like a group blowjob where one person fellates any number of others. As such, at the end of *The Justice League*, Wonder Woman (played by Chanel Preston) rewards the rest of the Super Friends for a crisis well averted. But rather than feeling secure in my safety and happy for the fellas, this particular scenario left an unpleasant taste in my mouth.

Pun not intended.

Although I maintain, respect, and hope that every person involved with this particular scene chose to participate on the basis of what they felt was right for them, the sociologist in me wondered about the gender implications of Wonder Woman's going from super equal team member to piñata-style party favor, because that's exactly what happened. You see, this wasn't just a blowbang. It was a *hard* blowbang, and its intensity was totally out of place relative to the rest of the film.

Before its conclusion, *The Justice League* was a fun, sexy parody. And in another genre or context, the mechanics of this particular sloppy gagging mess would've been fine, but here it seemed both mean-spirited and excessive. And I confess that I formulated all of this within the context of Mr. Bad Apple's leadership and vision. Surely he was up to his regular shtick, putting Wonder Woman in her place and Chanel through her paces.

So in the end, I loved *Ass-Fucked* and hated *The Justice League*. Fine. But here's the bigger issue—why? Why did final scenes that were comparably "rough" ruin one film and make the other that much better?

Juxtapose my assessment of Joanna's robust anal with Chanel's intense blowbang. What I was saying was that *Ass-Fucked*'s conclusion was intense—so super intense, in fact, that I could imagine it being used as an example in some sort of anti-adult entertainment rhetoric. Ironically, however, to me, that was exactly the kind of mind-set that that scene didn't support. In my view, *Ass-Fucked* was actually an acme moment in feminist expression, partly *because* of the intensity that was displayed during its conclusion.

But then, almost in the same breath, I was troubled by the fact that Wonder Woman went from integral team member to fuck-toy party favor during *The Justice League*. Why was that over-the-top blowbang necessary, and what are the implications? Why was I able to see the positive dimensions associated with vigor and "extreme" sex in one scene but only the bad in another?

I got called out on this.

I received an insightful series of comments regarding my reaction to *The Justice League* from respected adult industry critic Don Houston. He interpreted the blowbang (and my reaction to it) a little differently than I. Here's some of what he had to say:

> Your biggest concern comes from the blowbang, and while I'm not typically a fan of them either (be they light and fluffy or hard as can be nasty), perhaps you're reading too much into it (or I, not enough). Chanel/WW are sexual dynamos capable of bringing all those men to their knees via oral alone. In the character of WW, she was raised on an island devoid of all men, straying forth due to the shrinking world's likelihood of impacting her home. The mythology behind

the Amazons aside, couldn't WW be of a frame of mind to "catch up for lost time" and what better partners than physically enhanced heroes; none of whom asked her to get the coffee (knowing they'd be laid out on their asses), take notes of their meetings, or otherwise place her in a subordinate role? That she took them on as an equal, maybe more than equal if you catch my drift, speaks to her superiority over most of them.[1]

Exactly.

Don did a better job with this film than I. His take on the scene and its potential implications center on empowering, rather than disempowering, women. Why can't Wonder Woman be in control of the blowbang situation or exploring something new, thus choosing to celebrate the conclusion of yet another adventure with a bevy of cocks? And why couldn't I see this?

As Don correctly pointed out, I'm not a fan of this type of scene. But blowbangs aside, I let my feelings about a specific sex depiction (and the person who directed it) shape my assessment in a negative manner. Why did I choose to disempower Chanel's creative choices by empowering Mr. Bad Apple's? In other words, why couldn't Chanel be just as down for her scene as Joanna was for hers?

Don's perspective on this made me think a lot, especially when considering *The Justice League* in conjunction with *Ass-Fucked*. I was blown away by Joanna's bold bravado in *Ass-Fucked*—not my personal cup of tea, but incredible in so many ways. What's more, I was simultaneously concerned that a less-than-informed misreading of this scene might possibly diminish Joanna's autonomy and power. At the same time, even though I acknowledged the fact that everyone had to be on board for the final scene in *The Justice League*, all I could see were the negative implications of that Super Friends super fuck. I neglected to even consider, much less offer, another perspective or a different read-ing. It's certainly possible for both Wonder Woman and Chanel herself to like that blowbang, and the likelihood of her so doing (empower-ing) is no greater or less than my take (fairly disempowering). And this was informed wholly and completely by Mr. Bad Apple and the context I associated with him.

So essentially, I did to *The Justice League* exactly what I was afraid might happen to *Ass-Fucked*—I slipped down the slope of subjectiv-ity and offered up a potentially misread, limited interpretation shaped largely by personal bias and a particular agenda. In other words, I ass-fucked that blowbang, and not in a good way.

I still don't like that particular scene in *The Justice League*. I still think it was out of place, nasty, and unnecessary. In my view, it ruined the entire film. But I really appreciated the eye-opening reminder that Don's points initiated: No matter how much you know or think you know, all assessments are subjective. Even yours. Even mine.

10

"Tranny," Queer, and Tales of Loaded Language

IN LIFE, HOWEVER FOLKS WANT TO BE REFERRED TO, that's what I want to say. Whether it's a matter of a person's name or sex or gender or age or ethnicity or whatever, I support everyone's right to self-identify. But I struggle with the term "tranny," used frequently in mainstream porn to refer to women performers labeled male at birth who are often still in possession of a penis but are outwardly female in every other respect. It sounds so pejorative to me.

My discomfort with "tranny" is my own issue, a likely product of feminist and social justice-based research, advocacy work, and training—more theory than you can imagine and years and years of working with members of transgender and queer communities. In my subjective view, which has been informed by a wealth of particular personal experiences, "tranny" is not okay. But that doesn't mean everyone agrees with me. Nor does it mean that my position is correct.

But I keep thinking about it—"tranny"—often within the context of sex, gender, and porn.

For the sake of simplicity, let's consider sex and gender first. Sex has to do with your physical body, while gender has to do with your social expression of a range of masculinities and/or femininities (and/or neutralities). There are endless combinations of sex and gender by which a person may be labeled and may identify. The most important thing to remember though, in my opinion, is that people are entitled to identify as they choose.

Your assigned sex and/or gender may align with how you actually identify. That is cisgender. Cisgender refers to folks for whom the sex and gender they were assigned at birth, their bodies, and their personal identity all line up in a conventional (read: generally occurring) way. So, for example, I am a cisgender woman. I was assigned the sex female at birth and was raised as a girl. Today, I identify as an adult woman who is in possession of a female body—what I was labeled with as a young person matches up with what I feel I am today.

Your assigned sex and/or gender, however, may not align with how you actually identify. That is transgender. Transgender refers to folks whose gender identity and/or expression do not line up with their assigned physical sex and/or gender in a conventional way. So for example, a young person may be assigned female at birth and be raised as a girl, while identifying as a boy or (eventually) a man. This unconventional (read: less generally occurring) combination may prompt a person to identify as transgender.

Got it? Good! Let's go back to "tranny," a sex- and gender-related attribution and identity, within the context of porn.

Juxtaposing "tranny porn" with "queer porn" is useful. Consider the following passage, quoted from an early draft of an academic paper I published in 2014:

Reclaimed and highly charged, the term "queer" is both a descriptor of sexual orientation and a radical political positionality. The term's multi-faceted meaning applies to queer porn content as well. Generally, queer porn features performers of various gender identities and sexual orientations intermixing and exploring genres in ways infrequently seen in other sexually explicit content. For example, a queer porn narrative may feature transgender performers in a "conventional" romance. Also political, queer porn seeks to present a level of sexuality and identity authenticity (allegedly) absent from most other adult content.[1]

Let's talk about the term *queer* for a moment. Like "tranny," queer can be a hot-button word. It originally meant strange or unusual, but somewhere around 1900, queer morphed into a slur against gay men and perceived sexual deviance. And there it sat for almost one hundred years. Sometime during the 1990s though, members of the gay community started taking queer back—kinda like a "fuck you" to folks who had used the term against them. Consequently, the reappropriated term, which now refers to individuals who identify beyond gender binaries (for example, something other than man or woman) and/or heteronormative categorizations (for example, something other than cisgender heterosexual), came with both a radical political positionality and some controversy.

You see, though many folks embrace this identity, others simply do not care to be queer. Some people are just not political, or maybe they come from a place where the cruelty associated with the word is too much to get around. Or perhaps they know that not everyone who uses the word is trying to be nice or empowering. These concerns are absolutely legitimate, and they partially shape the way queer is engaged in the wider social word. Unfortunately though, when an understanding of something comes entirely from an academic and/or activist standpoint (as mine once did), one might forget about real-world harshness and these less-than-pleasant moments. This happened to me once regarding queer.

I had been invited to speak about the use of mainstream marketing tactics in adult novelty product sales at an industry-centered trade conference—beautiful sociology in practice. Approximately fifty brick-and-mortar retailers were to be in attendance; and considering the state I was in (California), the nature of the business I was engaging (sex toys), and the fact that it was then 2011, I felt confident addressing what I felt was a fairly simple point. Among other observations, I noted that, within their communities, buyers will be loyal to businesses that resonate with their identities, their interests, their needs, and so on. I made the point about women, about racially and ethnically diverse and/or concentrated communities, and about queer folks. (Of course, intersectionality[2] also comes into play.)

The first time I said "queer," I noticed a woman in the audience blink hard and start rustling around. I didn't think much of it, but the second time I said it, she stood up and demanded, "Stop it. Stop saying that word!"

I was completely taken aback, as was just about everyone else in the room. "What word?" I asked.

"'Queer'—you can't say that!"

"Ummm . . ." I was shocked into silence but quickly realized what was happening. "The term 'queer' has actually been reclaimed," I explained. "It's an empowering word meant to show support for all LGBT people . . . and for allies and for anyone else who chooses it."

"Well I'm bisexual, and it offends me! I don't want to hear it!" She was still standing. And shouting.

At this point, another woman from the crowd piped up: "Haven't you heard of Reel Queer Productions? Or Good Vibrations? They're right there in San Francisco, right in the middle of everything, and they say 'queer.'"

I took the opportunity to jump back in: "Look, I absolutely did not mean to offend you, but everything that I know, have seen, and have worked on tells me that this word is okay in this context." Then, to the entire room, "Let's get back to it! So the point I was trying to make was. . . ."

Yikes.

I sought the woman out after my talk was done. She was still beside herself, and no amount of explaining or offering references seemed to help. Eventually, she stormed off. I was nearly in tears. The idea that what I had said could be misinterpreted in such a way was absolutely mortifying. No one else seemed to have a problem though. One of her coworkers came up to me and said, "She's just like that." Reactionary with no filter, I guessed. Another young man, who let me know he was "soooo queer," gave me a bottle of fancy lube from his store, with wishes to have a better afternoon.

I still felt bad though.

Regarding language, within the context of my training as an academic and my work as a social justice advocate, everything I knew told me queer was okay. But what's clear from this example is that even though queer has been reclaimed, its meaning is not universal. For some, the term is still highly charged *in a negative way*. Just like the way "tranny" is for me. So let's go back to that academic paper of mine. This passage is about "tranny porn":

> Aside from featuring performers of various gender identities and sexual orientations, tranny (hereafter referred to as TS) content does not overlap with queer porn in any way. TS scenes generally

feature at least one performer who is in the midst of a male-to-female (MTF) transition. TS performers are generally partnered with cisgender men or other MTF TS performers, though I have recently noticed a slight increase in cisgender women performers working in TS scenes.[3]

To those not versed in gender, identity, and sexuality issues, there may be a lot going on here. And obviously there's more to all of this than could ever be explained in a few paragraphs, but put simply: Queer porn is different from all other genres of adult content because it's overtly political and social-justice minded. Within the context of sex work and performance, queer porn seeks to challenge our culture's conventional status quo. TS content, on the other hand, is generally not political. It's actually just like any other genre of porn that emphasizes some sort of sexual proclivity, taste, or fetish. Though myriad messages and themes may also be incorporated (as is the case with all porn), "tranny porn" is first and foremost about the entertainment, the fucking, and the performers doing it.

I once asked my friend Mr. D about these cross-genre structural similarities. Mr. D is an interesting and insightful individual, an adult content connoisseur in his private life and an adult industry professional in his public. As part of his job, Mr. D screens adult content, including "tranny porn" (as he also refers to it), for public relations purposes and production errors. I wondered about the patterns he had noticed during all this watching. His response was interesting and complex:

> First, the most noticeable thing is that the majority of transsexuals (at least those performing in the adult films I've seen) appear to be either Asian or Hispanic. Also for the most part, the TS performers

involved are on the receiving end—they do not do the penetrating. Besides that, TS porn is very similar to mainstream porn in regards to how a scene breaks down. The standard formula remains—fondling to oral to a variety of positions to the pop shot.[4]

So, Mr. D substantiated my assessment. In terms of production, TS content is structurally similar to mainstream porn. This is important. It's also important to notice Mr. D's use of "tranny," TS, and transsexual, all basically in the same breath.

In my observations, "tranny" is the attribution used most frequently by performers featured in TS scenes, by TS content producers, and by TS content consumers. Other commonly, but less frequently, used names include TS (which is obviously the term I feel most comfortable with), transsexual, and "shemale" (a term that makes me so uncomfortable that we're just gonna set it aside for now). All these terms, incidentally, come from within the TS portion of the adult entertainment community. So when I question and/or feel discomfort with one of these chosen attributions, I also feel a bit like I'm trying to come in and make others' struggles my own. The sociologist in me would call this an instance of colonizing or appropriation.

Like queer, "tranny" also has a tumultuous history punctuated with contempt. Unlike "tranny," though, queer has been reappropriated by many members of the population it once disparaged. Except that that's not entirely true. Many folks from various communities, including TS individuals, use the word "tranny" quite enthusiastically (and many people debate and reject this usage). So really, there are only two definitive things I can say about these words: (1) Both "tranny" and queer have variable meanings; and (2) I'm okay with queer, but I feel uncomfortable with "tranny." Thus, in my view, queer porn appears to be an empowering, chosen phrase, while "tranny porn" does not. Consequently, I constantly wonder why people who desire TS performers, employ and otherwise work with TS performers, or are themselves TS performers continue to say "tranny."

Maybe it's because "tranny" is what's familiar or recognizable. Could it be that people see that phrase and know immediately what they're getting? Maybe it's less about the problematic term and more about what's inside the proverbial box? This may be the case, as I've heard arguments along these lines from all sorts of folks directly connected to TS porn production, including TS performers. But then, is this okay? To me, it sounds way more like a "have to" than a choice.

"Tranny." It just seems wrong to me, but questioning folks' chosen identifiers is wrong, too!

I've been stockpiling TS porn for years now, and occasionally I try to make some sense of my ever-growing collection. I always get caught up in these mind-boggling, socio-social-justice linguistic and gender identity go-rounds, though. What's more, for the past couple of years, I have attended the "Tranny Awards"[5]—a ceremony dedicated specifically to TS women performers and the consumers who love them. I'm always super excited to learn more about this less visible but extremely vibrant segment of the adult community. Plus, it's always interesting to compare similar events catering to different dimensions of the industry, especially in light of occasional controversy occurring at other ceremonies.

For example, one year, some TS performers claimed that a large, more general awards-granting organization was discriminating against them. They alleged that they were not permitted to walk the red carpet (that was perhaps circumstantial as the red carpet at this event runs on a very strict timeline), and they correctly pointed out that awards honoring TS performers were not presented with significant fanfare. After some back and forth, adjustments were made, and the

Transsexual Performer of the Year award is now announced on stage alongside its Male Performer of the Year and Female Performer of the Year counterparts.

Pushback and change, yes, but there are still the same linguistic issues with variability and deciding who defines what.

As I said before, the most important thing to remember in all of this is that people are entitled to identify as they choose. And I need to accept that, in spite of what particular language may or may not make me uncomfortable. Ultimately, if folks want the Tranny Awards and tranny porn, then the Tranny Awards and tranny porn they shall have! I will continue to mull over it anxiously, though.

Without speaking to folks directly, there is no way to character- ize individuals accurately. So until you ask or you're informed about a preference, there's no way to know if a person identifies as a TS porn star, a transgender woman, a queer female, a tranny, a cisgender man, all of these, none of them, or something else entirely. What matters most is freedom of identity and expression.

11

Pegging: The Oldest New Trick in the Book

FOR FOLKS IN THE KNOW, THE ADULT VIDEO NEWS (AVN) Awards show is considered the highlight of each year's Adult Entertainment Expo (well, in a fading-supernova-mixed–with-industry-politics sort of way).

Often referred to as the "Oscars of Adult [Entertainment]," the AVN Awards are among the industry's highest accolades. They've been presented annually by the trade magazine since 1984, honoring work in production (e.g., Best POV Release), individual body of work (e.g., Best New Starlet), specific performance (e.g., Best Three-Way Sex Scene—Boy/Boy/Girl), marketing, technical, and specialty categories. There are numerous specific awards within each category—truly, an unwieldy amount—that seem to multiply, disappear or reappear, and shift each year.

I have served as an AVN Awards judge since 2010. It's an extremely daunting task. Judges have to watch everything, and "everything" is always a lot of content. The nominations are generally announced in early December, and companies begin shipping DVD screeners soon after. Some days the number of boxes arriving is so great they literally obstruct my front door. Not surprisingly, the judging process takes up a lot of time during what's already a pretty busy season. This, incidentally, means that I've watched porn in more than one airport. Being a judge is also unpaid and basically thankless. But I continue to volunteer my time in this way because I believe in recognizing the creative work that goes into all aspects of adult content production.

Some people like to complain about the awards' nomination and judging process. It's fixed, they say. The same people win over and over again, blah, blah, blah. I always find this a bit frustrating because, though I don't doubt that over the years there've been people who have bent the rules, I know that I take the entire thing very seriously. I've even developed my own viewing and voting system. It makes things far more manageable. First, I figure out which titles have the most nominations. Then, I gather up the other films or scenes that have also been designated alongside these "most frequent" noms for each respective award. Finally I watch. And take notes. And rate each nominee on the basis of several relevant criteria. By the time I'm done with this process, I've covered a lot of ground, but there's always more. So, regardless of my best efforts, any semblance of order falls by the wayside toward the end, especially when some companies send you their content weeks late!

It's a lot of work, but I love it. And though I struggle somewhat with awards in the technical category (Best Editing?), I love getting to see the best of everything—the blockbusters, the star showcases, and the newest installments in long-running serials. My favorites, though, are always the specialty awards. Because with categories like Best BDSM Release, MILF Release, and Best Transsexual Release, how could you not love 'em?

The darling of the specialty awards, in my opinion, hands down, is Clever Title of the Year. Sometimes funny, often in poor taste, and occasionally kinda mean, these titles are generally not the "best" releases in any one category. Usually, they just have catchy monikers. In 2012, for example, the nominees included *Bust a Nut or Die Tryin'*, *Sweaty College Girl Butt Stinky Panties*, *I Want You to Make My Mouth Pregnant*, and *Beggin' for a Peggin'*, among many others.

The winner of 2012's Clever Title of the Year award, however, was not my choice. My vote went to *I Want You to Make My Mouth Pregnant*, but the winner was *Beggin' For A Peggin'*.

Here's the film's quite useful synopsis, quoted from the box copy:

> As the Urban Dictionary describes it, pegging is the sexual scenario in which "the tables are voluntarily turned on heterosexual anal intercourse and the female services the man with a strap-on dildo." And while pegging has been a part of popular culture since Gore Vidal wrote about it in *Myra Breckinridge*, you can now see it performed by some of adult entertainment's hottest stars in the taboo-bustin' new Reality Blue Media release *Beggin' For A Peggin'*. . . . Once you see what these girls can deliver, you'll be "beggin' for a peggin'" too!

Now, despite my earlier comments and what generally occurs with the Clever Title of the Year nominees, *Beggin'* was not just a flashy, all-sass/no-substance title. The same year, *Beggin'* also won the creative technical award for Best Fem-Dom Strap-On Release. And whoever wrote the film's synopsis is indeed correct: Pegging has been around for quite a while. *Myra Breckinridge* was published in 1968, so the practice goes back at least that far. You can also find pegging scenes in the earliest professional adult content productions. Case in point: *The Opening of Misty Beethoven*, from 1975, has a prosthetic-enhanced scene in which the Misty character has her guy's needs . . . pegged. And, also just like *Beggin'*, there's more to *Misty Beethoven* than might first meet the eye.

Misty Beethoven is an adult take on a mainstream literary classic, George Bernard Shaw's play *Pygmalion*. Suave Dr. Love endeavors to transform the jaded and passionless "sexual civil service worker" Misty Beethoven into an elite, erotic "it" girl. By the end of the film, however, the tables have turned. Misty has become the trainer, and Dr. Love has become her subservient.

Here's something I wrote about the pegging scene in *Misty Beethoven* in "From *The Devil in Miss Jones* to *DMJ6:*"

> Generally, the sex depictions in *Misty Beethoven* epitomize content of the Reel Era [of adult content production, 1957–1975], however the film does contain one depiction that is both extreme for the era and extreme within the context of the entire sample. During the film's third sex scene, the woman lead character is shown penetrating a man character's anus with a strap-on prosthetic while he penetrates a second woman's vagina. Although three-way sex depictions involving a man and two women are fairly standard fare in the adult films informing this discussion, no other scene in this sample contains depictions similar to those in this scene. This particular depiction both destabilizes adult film sex depiction scripts and presumptions about heteronormative sex behaviors within the context of this sample while simultaneously reifying a consistent heteronormative cultural taboo.[1]

So a woman starts out being "remade" in a very heteronormative[2] way, only to end up remaking heteronormativity herself. That's interesting! And it's also interesting to consider what a strong presence pegging had back in the earliest days of adult. Because even though this was only one scene in one film, it was still a significant part of a very high-profile title. Relatively, pegging in *Misty Beethoven* was a big deal.

Nevertheless, pegging seemed to disappear quickly. When I was writing about *Misty Beethoven* in "*DMJ6*," I had a hard time figuring out what pegging was actually even called. The pegging genre hadn't quite resurged back then. What's more, pegging is not even directly referred to in that "*DMJ6*" paper. When I was researching and writing it, the nomenclature had become so obscure that I couldn't find a citation or attribution considered "legitimate" enough to hold water in an academic paper. So I describe the pegging that occurs in *Misty Beethoven*, but the term itself is not present. It was edited out during the peer-review process.

But pegging does exist! It always has. And even though you may not have seen much pegging in mainstream, or even fringe, adult content during the eighties, nineties, or early 2000s, pegging is making a major comeback today. Case in point: the aforementioned *Beggin' For A Peggin'*. In the film, "her fantasy becomes his reality. . . ."

Beggin' For A Peggin' features five fairly big-deal women performers (a sure sign of mainstreaming) pegging five variably known dudes: Francesca Le with Christian XXX; Jewels Jade with Gabriel D'Alessandro; Aiden Starr with Tom Moore; Chanel Preston with Jason Katana; and Kristina Rose with Christian XXX again. In each scene, we get a bit of slightly awkward-seeming fem-dommey play (which is understandable since fem-domme is the foremost forte of only one of these women performers), some traditional fucking, and then the pegging. Throughout, the dudes appear to be super happy. The women are into it, as well. It's uplifting.

And the sociological implications are huge. Just as in *Misty*

Beethoven, heteronormativity is destabilized—but now in contemporary times with well-known performers in an increasingly popular genre. People want this kind of porn, so producers and performers respond with time and energy and products. *Beggin'* and films like it are important because they are evidence of society's shifting ideals about gender and sexualities.

A lot of sociologically interesting commentary also happens during the film's behind-the-scenes footage. Filmmakers interview some of the peggin' gals about what it's like to fuck a dude with a strap-on, in some instances for the very first time. I found this absolutely fascinating, both because it violates a key performers' Golden Rule—never let your first time doing anything be on camera—and reveals a measure of sexual inexperience. Evidently, porn performers don't just naturally know how to do everything sexual.

I was very appreciative of the opportunity to watch this film and others like it. It allowed me to expand my own, somewhat stunted, experiences exploring the pegging genre. And it really got me thinking about changing trends in sex depictions, what's popular, what's mainstream, what's acceptable, and everything in between.

This type of thing is just one of the reasons why I love being an AVN Awards voter.

12

Beyond Porn Funk

I'VE ALWAYS BEEN VERY MUSICAL. MY PARENTS MADE SURE of that. Both of them were always into all different kinds of music, my dad being more country and classic rock oriented and my mom more into metal and emerging/edgy. She was responsible for introducing me to several artists who have since shaped dimensions of my entire life, from Guns N' Roses to Concrete Blonde. When my brothers and I were young, we all had music lessons of some sort. And though I did go through an embarrassing preteen New Kids on the Block stage, my first real concert was an Ozzy Osbourne/Black Sabbath/Sepultura show at an outdoor amphitheater in Los Angeles. My parents took me.

Not surprisingly, I grew into quite the adolescent metalhead. From Megadeth to Pantera and everything in between—even Tesla and Cinderella—I was into it. And having been a teenager in the nineties, I'm still and always forever grunge. Somewhere in that mix, I also developed a great love for Tool, music beyond description that allowed me secret segues into other genres.

In college I grew to have a deep love of cheesy radio funk and LA-based Latin hip-hop. You could always find me at some county fair where a Gap Band revival was playing, and I used to go hear Ozomatli every Tuesday night back when they were the house band at the Dragonfly. The uncommon imagery of Modest Mouse still slays me, and then there were those forty-odd Fishbone shows I attended all across the entire LA basin.

Eventually, as I became more of an adult, I started to appreciate what I used to think of as "girl music"—Neko Case and Sleater-Kinney, Björk and Bikini Kill, Selena and Dolly Parton, and so many others—brilliant women artists whom I didn't appreciate until I was into my twenties.

And since then, so many more significant influences have only added to the brilliant tapestry of music I've been so lucky to behold—music in Texas, music in New York, music in small mountain towns in Arizona. I'll spare you further name drops though and leave you with just two words: The Shins.

Given all this, it's not surprising that when I was looking for a "for-fun" side research project between completing my dissertation and my years as a visiting scholar at the University of Southern California (USC, 2012–2013)—you know, in my infinite free time between researching gender and law and occupational structures shaping adult entertainment—I settled on music in porn. I had actually been interested in this for a while, in part because of an annoying thing that often happened when I told people about my work.

When people asked me about what my sociological endeavors entailed, depending on who they were, they'd get one of two answers. For people I perceived to be more conservative, I studied "occupational structures and workers' rights in stigmatized yet legal industries operating in the United States." Generally, this was obscure enough to get people to zone out and stop asking questions. For those who seemed more open-minded, I studied "the sociocultural significance of adult entertainment as it relates to law, media, and gender." Almost invariably, option two would prompt the response: "Adult entertainment? Wait! You mean porn? *Bow-chicka-bow-wowww*!" Apparently this sound effect is synonymous with adult content.

The thing is, though, that it isn't. Absent some golden-era films produced during the time when funk was at its popular height, you never really hear anything remotely *bow-chicka-bow-wow* in porn. At least, I haven't. So why does everyone think it's there? I had been curious about this question for a long while. Couple that with all of the really creative content producers I know—people who add thoughtful, occasionally original music to their porn—and my own long love affair with music, and I had another project on my hands.

I picked away at porno soundscapes for a while, tossing around ideas in my free time, asking questions when the topic came up, and paying attention to the noteworthy (and occasionally terrible) music I came across. I was trying to pull an interesting, specific question from yet another sea of misunderstanding. And though I wasn't trying too hard, I also wasn't having much luck. Then one day, a call for papers (CFP) from the Experience Music Project (EMP) museum came my way.

The EMP in Seattle is a "leading-edge" (their words), nonprofit space rooted in music and dedicated to the risk-taking ideas that fuel contemporary popular culture. They hold several regional conferences around the country each year, and 2013's Los Angeles–area meeting was dedicated to "Locals Only: Pop & Politics in This Town." The CFP asked for work pertaining to music, media, gender, and insiders/outsiders in LA. It took me all of an eighth of a second to come up with "music, media, locals yet still outsiders—porn!" It was a great opportunity to work through some ideas and get some points in with my department at USC, which was where the conference was being held. A little bit of finessing yielded this submission:

Beyond "Porn Funk"—Sociocultural Evolutions of Music in Adult Content, Past and Present

Although all types and forms of pornography are created around the globe, the professional adult content production industry is unique to Los Angeles, specifically to the San Fernando Valley. Interestingly, the music scoring porn has often been regarded as "cheesy," ancillary, or even unnecessary. This important dimension of adult content production, however, is anything but insignificant. Like all media (and all aspects of this media specifically), music in porn has evolved in conjunction with wider sociocultural evolutions and with changes within the adult industry itself. In this talk, I will outline the historical development of music scoring adult content from the 1970s through today. Further, I will engage insights gleaned from in-depth interviews with five currently influential and active adult content producers and/or directors in order to explore the significance of contemporary music in porn.

My proposal was accepted immediately, and the organizers commended me for my creativity. I was excited. I got to work.

On the day of the conference, I showed up pumped to present my findings. The project had changed shape some since my original proposal, but I was confident about it. Outlining the development of the music that scored adult content from the 1970s through the present—a dissertation-size ethnomusicology endeavor—had proven to be a bit too much for the occasion. I had scaled the scope of the project back but had still been able to incorporate a touch of historical depth.

Funk music emerged in the 1960s and was originally associated with the Black Power Movement. It then moved through wider culture, reaching a high point in the 1970s before all but disappearing by the 1980s. And somehow, since then, it's become synonymous with porn, sparking yet another legacy of social and cultural "knowledge" that is widely misinformed. That was as far as I had gotten, choosing instead to focus my energies on a smaller question: How does mythology of "porn funk" measure up against the real, contemporary world of music in adult content production?

In order to explore my refined query, I conducted in-depth interviews with fourteen current adult content producers and directors (four women and ten men, whose experience in the industry ranged from two to forty years). I talked to great people: Barrett Blade, Jonni Darkko, Eddie Powell, and Jacky St. James, among others. I learned that, during the recent industry downturn, as financial constraints have tightened around professional adult content production, especially feature-length projects, music has become even less of a priority. (Outside the work of some auteurs, porn has generally always been more about the visual depiction of sex and less about other aspects of production, like music.) Consequently, the vast majority of music used in contemporary content is pulled almost arbitrarily from licensed catalogues or libraries. Most of the time very little thought is put into the process. But in some instances, I found that one of three other options occurred: (1) Producers were imaginative and culturally aware with their use of catalogue music; (2) Producers complemented thoughtful catalogue selections with some original music; or (3) Producers occasionally used porn as *the* platform to produce completely new music.

Jacky St. James and Eddie Powell told me how they plumbed existing catalogues, seeking out classics and recognizable fair-use content that would connect to viewers on a deeper psychological level. Barrett Blade, a former professional musician, described how he would occasionally write original music for scenes and segments in his films, filling in places and spaces where catalogue content just didn't work. And Jonni Darkko, who at the time of our interview had created more than 150 films, wrote an original score for every single project. For him, porn was just a visual accompaniment to his preferred auditory art form.

I concluded my talk with my own musings—why, in spite of all this obviously thoughtful creativity, did people continued to *bow-chicka-bow-wow* porn to death? I had a few theories: In addition to there actually being a fair measure of lazy, stereotyped "porny" music out there, (1) Unfamiliarity breeds reliance on stereotypes; (2) Our wider culture is generally uncomfortable with sex; and (3) It has something to do with sociologist Jean Baudrillard's ideas about a copy of a copy of a copy (and so on) losing its original integrity.[1]

My ideas were smart, people asked good questions, and I got a lot of great feedback. A few weeks later, I had a final research article ready for peer-reviewed journal submission. Why the hell not, right?

I sent the manuscript off to my first-choice journal, and my article was promptly rejected. Not offered notes and a "revise and resubmit"—just rejected. Not provided with the name of a more appropriate journal—rejected. I tried another, then another. Three different journals, three rejections without comment. I said, "Fuck it" and moved on, but I was more than a little disappointed. And in spite of everything academic I had already been through, I was surprised. About a year later, I saw a CFP from an area studies journal asking for papers on music in porn. I tried to control my frustration as I read my own ideas reflected almost verbatim in the call.

Six months before that, however, I ran into one of the women I had interviewed for the project. It was the first time I had seen her since we'd talked, and she immediately thanked me. She had listened to the live audio webcast of my presentation and was touched by how poignantly I had captured the meaning of music in her work. She wanted to make sure I knew that I had gotten it correct.

A while later, after she had gone on her way and I was alone, I sat down, head in hands and shoulders low. Though the cursory dismissals still stung, it no longer mattered that my porn funk paper had been rejected three times without comment. It didn't matter that all the big thinkers of the world would never know or care about the significance of this director's work. It didn't matter that no "legitimate" forum would publish my research, and it didn't matter that the CFP had reflected my ideas without reference or citation—at least, it didn't anymore. What truly mattered was that there had been a space for her voice.

I thought about all this and I thought about her gratitude, and I cried—great, exhausted, forever frustrated, but never-to-be-beaten tears. Again.

13

The Power of the P(orn Fans)

IT COULD HAVE BEEN ANY EVENT, AS LONG AS IT WAS ONE where fans were present. I was standing off to the side of the slightly raised stage area, behind a row of women signing autographs—one of my many posts. I was far enough away to be unobtrusive but close enough to hear what was going on, ready to intercede if necessary.

It had already been hours, and the crowd in front of the booth was thick, always on the verge of closing in tighter. There was no easy way out, and we were all a bit on edge. Audrey Bea's beauty was on high beam, like a sacrificial mermaid at the front of a ship. She glanced my way, and her silent scream—*holymarymotherfuckingshit, I cannot stand this!*—was visible in the almost imperceptible wince of her lower lash line.

I met her gaze and attempted to send her some telepathic reassurance—*Hang in there, honey! Your shift is almost up*—when I was yanked hard to the right and nearly knocked off my feet by Destiny Rain.

"This guy is . . . *wet!?* Get him off me!" Destiny hissed under her breath. Her nails dug into my arm as she used me as an anchor to pull

her body left, away from the meaty-looking gentleman on her opposite side. Her glossy smile never flickered, not even once.

"Sir, you're gonna have to move along now," I said, as I scooted
around and wedged myself in between her and him. He was, in fact,
quite wet. "There are lots of other people here who want to see Ms.
Destiny, too."

The line never got any shorter.

"Ugh, every year, the same crap. He's such a fan," Akeela Song
lamented to no one in particular. When a porn star referred to someone being "such a fan" like Akeela had, they were talking about a
certain type of admirer—one who had crossed the line of appropriate and had drifted into starstruck or obsessive. But at that moment,
everything was okay. Akeela's signing shift was over, and it was time for
her to go. She tossed a pile of expensive gifts into a nearby garbage can
as she retreated to the interior of the booth.

As I kept one eye on Akeela, I could hear Krystal Harris biting back
at a fan who had gotten a little too pushy. "If I'm such a whore, then
why are you here? I didn't wait in line to see you," she pointed out the
obvious, her disdain apparent.

And as the days and years passed, time after time and show after
show, I found myself between star after star and her "biggest fan,"
someone who had waited hours for just one moment of attention—or
for the opportunity to ask her what her father thought of her. I ducked
through secret hallways in huge hotels, dragging suitcases and carrying everything from small dogs to cartoon-themed humidifiers, always
making sure to shield whatever charge or friend I was currently block-
ading from the strangest mix of human adoration and disgust. It was an
intoxicating yet toxic cocktail that eventually seemed to get them all.

I do not understand what happens to people when they become
porn fans.

I noticed it immediately, at the very first fan show I attended back in my intern days. People, some of whom seemed almost hypnotized by lust or joy or fascination, would wait for hours to meet their favorite starlet. Some would have gifts, occasionally even thoughtful ones. All of them wanted a picture. The performers would smile and preen and pose . . . and then, almost invariably, express their disgust in some small imperceptible way.

I was shocked. How could they be so dismissive of people who were, for all intents and purposes, the reason they were there? Without fans or consumers there would be no porn or fame—or any of the perks that went along with it.

But I realized pretty quickly that there was way more going on than just overt dismissal. The exchange between fans and performers was actually quite complex. It broke down like this: For every sincerely kind enthusiast, there were at least a hundred weirdos—salivating, grabbing, deep-breathing, occasionally wet, often creepy individuals who expected far too much attention during their allotted thirty seconds. There were also a handful of outright assholes—people who came with stacks of photos or product they expected signed, all so they could turn around and sell everything on eBay. (This was 2007.) There were also people who came with the express purpose of saying and asking mean things. "You've gotten a lot fatter since you were nineteen!" or "Do you think your kid and his friends ever watch you fuck? I bet that gangbang you did would really freak them out!" A lot of them actually expected a civil, thoughtful response.

And then there were the super fans. Rarer than the assholes, some of these folks were genuinely nice sorts who had just slipped a little too far into the fantasy. They knew intimate details and personal information, they remembered birthdays, they were pleasant and polite, but just beneath the surface they were also slightly unhinged. It was subtle and unsettling. Some super fans were openly raw and completely over the edge, the kind of people who made a woman's spine freeze when she saw them inching their way to the front of the line. The kind of people who sincerely believed they *knew* their favorite performer, and one day she would be theirs, no matter what.

The longer I watched—two hours, six hours, four days in a row, show after show—and the more times I had to tell an adult that he was not entitled to grope or hassle a woman simply because he had seen pictures of her naked, the more complex the relationship between performers and fans became. It's not that the performers were ungrateful, it's that they were tired. It's not that the performers were rude, it's that their non-camera-side shoulder was drenched in a slurry of others' BO. Some of them were better at maintaining their composure in these situations, but every single one of them walked away from a fan day feeling at least a little tender. Or so I've been told.

In recent years, social media specifically and the Internet in general have cranked this dynamic up to new levels. No longer do you have to leave your home to adore or berate your favorite performer—just reach out via Twitter! She may not respond, but she'll most likely see what you have to say. Want to give a special gift? Performers create wish lists just for you! Chances are you'll get a thank-you package from the recipient, or at least an image of her with the shoes, computer, body products, or sex toys you bought. And if you'd like to offer extended commentary, good or bad, on anything related to your favorite lady or her work, there are endless online forums. And most of the time, there will be other fans on there to interact with you.

When I first started exploring these dynamics, I was taken aback by how aggressive and entitled some fans seemed to be. Today, I'm taken aback by how much *more* aggressive and entitled even more of them have become. Just a few years ago it took a fair amount of effort to be weird, mean, or even nice; thus, fewer people seemed inclined to expend the energy. Today, we can throw out insults and compliments at the drop of a hat—hiding behind the computer, fishing for some sort of response, and feeling entitled to a meaningful interaction.

Imagine a Twitter user called @InventedXXXFan. In any five-minute period, @IXF may tweet some version of "You're so hot baby, can I get a RT?" to as many performers as possible, swapping out names and reproducing the oh-so-meaningful message. Presumably, this shotgun approach will yield a response or two. And if it doesn't, you can almost always see the same handle a little while later, this time with the missive, "Fuck you, you cock-sucking whore-slut!" undoubtedly rendered with some creative spelling and punctuation.

What is the point of this manic gimme-something-or-I'll-insult-you social media exchange? And why in the world would people expect a response?

Maybe because they occasionally get one. I've seen it more than once—from high-profile porn stars to new performers starting out, debating some keyboard warrior on a public forum. Women are compelled to defend their motherhood and their bodies. Performers argue the politics of their industry with people who are in no way connected to it or informed about its dealings. University students and individuals with advanced professional certifications—because some porn stars are also in college and some have earned any number of impressive accreditations—defend their intellect in light of their current chosen profession, all on nameless, faceless social media.

I read a news item once about a young girl who had tweeted to her mainstream celebrity boy-band crush something along the lines of, "Respond to me, or I will hurt this dog!" The message was accompanied with an image of her threatening a Chihuahua. And though the entire thing was later found to be a hoax, the boy-band crush, too popular to have ever even seen the image in a timely manner, never responded. But porn stars do respond. They respond to the insults, the kindnesses, and the requests for birthday shout-outs. Not always and not perfectly but far more frequently than their mainstream counterparts. This is because, in the current age of porn production, proof of a large fan base, as evidenced by a considerable social media following, provides an independent performer with bargaining power and creative control. Career negotiations aren't similarly impacted or improved for mainstream celebrities.

Like every other kind of entertainer since the dawn of time, porn performers are dependent upon their fans—all fans, even the cruel and inappropriate ones. And currently that's true in a new and increasingly significant way. Some devotees negotiate the boundaries and norms of fandom differently. Today's virtual world has blurred these boundaries, however, changing the nature of celebrity interaction.

The business of sex is a special case within this changing world. Professional commercial sex work seems to foster an odd, manufactured sense of intimacy in its consumers (and, occasionally, in its workers). Couple this with our wider social discomfort with sex, the stigma of sex work, and the very public nature of porn, and what you get is a perfect storm in which "Fuck you, whore! I love you, baby. . . . Now give me some free stuff" all come together in the same 140-character message.

14

Being a Guy in
Porn Is (Not) Hard

NO ONE EVER PAYS ATTENTION TO THE GUYS IN PORN.

Well, some people pay some attention to some of the guys who work as performers. Gay porn has produced a hefty handful of stars over the decades, and there's obviously the iconic Ron "The Hedgehog" Jeremy, who has worked in porn since the seventies and has more than 2,200 credits to his name. We also have that oh-so-topical panty-dropping juggernaut James Deen, and I've noticed more and more men performers getting quite a bit of fan-girl delight in recent years. Tommy Pistol, Xander Corvus, and Johnny Castle all garner their fair share of love.

But these examples are only a small fraction of the porno men who've come and gone. Though no one knows for sure—because the labor statistics don't exist—I've heard industry insiders, such as agents and people responsible for hiring, say there are anywhere from thirty to fifty guys working as porn performers at any given time. But this number is constantly in flux and doesn't take into account the fringe guys and the mopes[1] who, for example, fill in a gangbang and whose faces you never really see. These disembodied penises thrust in and out of scenes with nonexistent fanfare, all while even the most obscure lady performers get far more attention.

And when concerned activists or academics raise questions about fair and ethical workplaces and occupational fulfillment, it's always for the ladies. No one ever pays attention to the labor performed by the guys. Whether they're James Deen–caliber or some random amateur, no one asks if the work is fair, ethical, or fulfilling for them.

— x x x —

I was on set in the San Fernando Valley recently. This was not a big deal. As I said, I've been on many sets over the past ten or so years. From the most elaborate of productions to ratty apartments in North Hollywood shooting single-camera POV, I've seen it all.

The shoot that day was for a smaller project for a fairly well-known company. A director I'm close with had started a new series of vignette lines—collections of roughly thirty-minute mini-movies. The intent was to find a middle ground between all-sex collections and films with a longer narrative. I was curious to see the production process behind this resurging format, and there's always something to be learned about community and culture when you're a fly on the wall. And if nothing else, I could blog about it. So I went.

Two scenes were scheduled that day: a romantic interlude followed by a naughty/dirty stepsibling thing—"faux-cest," which happens to be wildly popular with consumers these days. Call time was 8 a.m. for the first scene, noon for the second. I was more interested in the taboo tenor of the faux-cest, so I planned on arriving around 12:30 p.m. That way, there would be time for a little chitchat before actual sexy time commenced.

But this was not to be the case.

The first scene should've been simple—a little bit of set-up dialogue before sex. No elaborate acrobatics, no looming pressure from the four-person crew (director, production assistant, camera guy, and photographer), and a pretty bedroom set in a beautiful, airy house. Nothing to it.

I received a call at around eleven. Things weren't going well, so could I please come closer to one? Everything had been pushed back. The director came charging out front as soon as I arrived at 1:15 (due to another scheduling adjustment). "We're just about to start sex," the director said, referring to the first scene. Only just now starting? Yikes! I quickly shifted gears in my head. I could not fathom staying on set for another fours hours after this, but what was there of interest in everyday romance when I had anticipated something far more edgy?

And what the heck was going on anyway? The woman in the morning's scene, Ginger Moore, was a tall, fresh redhead in her early twenties. Apparently, Ginger had been late. Way late. And then she was hungry. And then she didn't like her makeup. And then there were new performer problems, and then, and then. . . . "She's never gonna get booked again," I thought to myself. But, oh well. I'd never heard of her anyway.

Then I started thinking about her scene partner, Tyler Max. Tyler was beautiful—tall, clean cut, and decently jacked. He was well respected and well represented, though also known to display a little too much bravado on occasion. But he had more than ten years of performance experience and more than five hundred scene credits to his name, working in everything from difficult acting to the hardest of hardcore, so you kinda had to give it to him.

For this "straight boy-girl" (read: basic foreplay leading up to vaginal penetrative sex and an external pop), even though Tyler was seasoned and Ginger was new, he was still getting paid several hundred dollars less than her. Granted, he didn't have to cover all the hidden costs she did (e.g., wardrobe options and the extensive manicuring that ladies are expected to maintain to be camera ready), but he'd been on time. And five hundred scenes! He was proven. All I could think about was how long he'd already had to keep his dick hard that day, and things were just now (maybe) getting started.

I went inside the set house and assessed the situation. Where would I be the least intrusive? The large, open room was split by a false wall. The set was on one side, while a couch on the other provided a perfect vantage point. It would be easy to hear from there, and a conveniently located mirror near the door allowed for a crystal-clear view of the action. I stationed myself a mere fifteen feet from people work-fucking without creating even the tiniest interruption and began taking notes. I was still trying to figure out what I was going to do with the documentation.

A little dog hopped up on the cushions and curled alongside me. Adorable. The next scene's performers arrived, just as quietly as I had. Edgy-looking Ms. Bad Girl began contemplating outfits brimming from her huge suitcase. In an effort to pass the time, ordinary every-guy Richard Roe went outside to juggle bowling pins. Inexplicably, an agent showed up, too.

Nothing of real consequence was happening on the other side of the wall. I mean, sex was happening, but it was nothing out of the ordinary. At one point, I glanced up into the mirror and saw Tyler making romantic love to Ginger from behind. She still had her panties on, which he held aside with one hand. It was kinda hot . . . temperature-wise. The director was giving instructions, moving the scene along—flip this way, look that way, and so on. There were occasional breaks for hardcore stills.

And then it was time. Pop time.

The crew gathered around. The photographer came out to my side of the wall. Everyone else went about their business. The little dog yawned. So did I.

But all of a sudden, there was a problem. Everyone stopped. It was too hot inside with no air-conditioning, and the day had been too long. Our cocksmith couldn't get to the grand finale. The crew drifted out as the performers cooled off and reheated on the other side of the wall. I could hear Ginger trying to nurse Tyler back to life as I chatted quietly with the photographer. The director and the production assistant began some paperwork; the camera guy took a few hits off his e-cig.

Then suddenly, Tyler announced: "I'm ready." He's ready! Mad dash to places everyone!

But again, it was too hot and had been too long of a day. The director talked to the agent, the production assistant went back to his paperwork, the camera guy went back to his e-cig.

Then again, "I'm ready." He's ready! Mad dash to places everyone!

And again, it was too hot and had been too long of a day. The production assistant brought in an oscillating fan, which only succeeded in blowing sex and heat around the rest of the room. The director gave Ms. Bad Girl feedback on her outfit, as the agent left. Richard was still outside; the camera guy went back to his e-cig.

Then another, "I'm ready." Mad dash to places everyone!

And once again, the same story. The director started attending to Ginger, who actually was being remarkably helpful from what I could tell. Tyler was getting apologetic and anxious, and the production assistant (PA) was getting impatient. He was pacing around, throwing out insulting little jabs, and talking about the baseball game he'd be attending later that day. That seemed counterproductive. He eventually went into the refrigerator and cracked a beer, much to Tyler's chagrin.

"Hey, man, sorry," said the PA. "You can have one too, but only if you pop."

I started writing down times as the cycle repeated itself: 2:31, 2:42, 2:49. . . . The production assistant, now looking to salvage the scene as best he could, offered Tyler some options: "You can keep fucking her or you can beat it. I don't care, just as long as you cum."

Finally—mercifully—at 3:01, the entire crew decided they needed to simulate the scene's culmination. They knocked out three options: a Cetaphil splatter (Cetaphil or something similarly milky and white is the liquid of choice for a fake external pop in porn) from off-camera, a soft shot of a fake internal vaginal pop, and a fake internal blowjob pop (using coconut oil this time, not cleanser). Everything was complete by 3:27.

Ginger bounced into the shower, all giggles and smiles and tropical sheen. The crew scrambled around to change out the set. Ms. Bad Girl and Richard flirted softly in the corner of the room. And as I took my leave, I noticed Tyler's reflection in the mirror. Still butt-ass naked, sweaty, and chiseled, he was standing with his head bowed. He looked broken-hearted and embarrassed. Word of today's non-performance would get around quickly, and you're only as good as your last scene.

— x x x —

A few days later, I followed up with the director. "That scene sucked, the second one was sooo much better," they lamented. In the midst of an absolutely unnecessary apology, it was also mentioned that Tyler had voluntarily discounted his rate that day, meaning he was paid even less. You know, because he didn't finish the job.

No one ever pays attention to the guys in porn.

15

Match Mates

I MET KELLE DASH SOMETIME AROUND 2008. IN THOSE days, Kelle appeared to be climbing to the top of her game, two steps away from having it all. In reality though, she was going through some sort of a transition.

Almost all successful people are hustlers, and Kelle was and is no exception. Stunningly pretty, she started out trying to be a conventional mainstream model in the early 2000s. Then she became a bikini model, then a topless model, then a nude model. Then she started doing entry-level gonzo[1] porn. Some might have said she was hustling in the wrong direction.

Almost immediately after shooting her first few adult scenes, Kelle caught the eye of a renowned performer/director. They fell in love, and he introduced her to all the right people—people who, coincidentally, happened to be looking for something new and noteworthy. The adult industry was hitting a bit of a slump, and top producers were on the lookout for *it*—the next big something that would get consumers to buy. What no one wanted to acknowledge, though, was that the proliferation of free, pirated content on tube sites had already taken hold.

Tube sites have been a bane on the adult entertainment industry since the mid-2000s. And though no one was really talking about their impact when I first met Kelle, no one was really buying anything either.

But this didn't keep producers from attempting to work within the frame of their previously tried and true methods. They were looking for something new and shiny, and Kelle was exceptionally so. She and her guy got married just weeks before she signed an exclusive performance contract with a well-respected company. Back then, this was the porn star equivalent of winning the lottery, an increasingly rare version of the Fairytale of (Almost) Effortless Success. When I met Kelle, she was only a few months into her new employment as an exclusive "contract girl" and totally on top of the world. Almost overnight, she had become one of a small handful of superstars in porn, complete with a prestigious brand at her back. She was working exclusively with her husband and other women in what were relatively creative erotic projects. And though she was a little high-maintenance and dramatic at times, she was also really fun and funny and smart. She cared about her family, loved her dog, and had a good heart. We became buddies.

As the months passed, Kelle's star continued to rise. She photographed beautifully, traveled extensively, and became a minor celebrity in a world where everyone was allegedly famous. One time, while we were waiting in line at a local burrito joint in the Valley, a young man not a day over twenty sidled up to her shyly. "Are you Kelle Dash?" he asked, barely audible and tremendously flushed. She smiled sweetly in return, which was all the response that was necessary. The young man managed to maintain his composure—and Kelle's eye contact—while thanking her for her work, which he loved.

It was really sweet. But not everything in Kelle's life was comparably smooth.

Though things on the surface looked great and her public persona was gaining momentum, things behind the scenes were coming unglued. Her penchant for drama had devolved into an anxiety-driven diva complex, and full-on meltdowns happened at the slightest provocation. Her increasing drug use didn't help either. Things were also going south in the romance department, and her marriage had gone from hot and heavy to down in flames. Eventually, all this began to affect her work. Kelle clashed with directors, other performers, and even her boss. In a fit of justifiable temper, she made a serious gaffe that ultimately cost her job. And then one day she got a letter from the IRS.

During one particularly rocky period, Kelle suggested we needed a ladies' weekend. She was booked to host a series of events at one of the then-hottest casinos in Las Vegas. In addition to all the standard party favors that came with such occasions, the venue was putting her up in their opulent new condo tower. Kelle and I, along with two other girlfriends, made a beeline for the desert, kicking off four days of ultra fun. Inevitably though, somewhere in the midst of pool parties and bubble baths, we all started talking about work.

One girlfriend, Ms. Director X, was a fairly prominent adult content producer. She was in the midst of developing a special project and wanted Kelle to be the star. And the best part was that Kelle could pick anyone—*anyone!*—she wanted to work with for this project, regardless of rate. There were no budgetary constraints.

"If you could pick anyone to work with, anyone at all, who would it be?" Ms. X asked Kelle.

My head started whirling. Who should she choose? I started weighing the options, as if I had some say.

But Kelle needed no time to think. She mused for approximately an eighth of a second before gushing—and I quote—"Oh my god, Manuel [Ferrara]![2] I've never worked with him before, and his penis is sooo perfect!"

This seemed to be an interesting, and rather opportune, prospect. For the past couple years, the only man Kelle had worked with, while shooting exclusively for one company, was her now-ex-husband. Being partnered with someone new and different, especially someone she was super excited about, within the context of an entirely new and different pornographic lens, might have a cleansing, refreshing effect—both on her emotions and on her career.

And so it was done: Manuel was cast, Kelle was elated (both before the scene was shot and after it was completed), and I got to thinking. Certainly Kelle was not unique. I mean, of course, she was a unique and special individual; but certainly other adult performers have a list of folks they'd just love to work with but haven't.

I was reminded of this several months later when UK-based production house Joybear Pictures sent me a screener for their film *Match Mates*. To this day, it's still one of the hottest, most original, and amazing films I've ever seen. In *Match Mates,* former producer and first-time director Liselle Bailey does something incredible. She plays matchmaker with her porn star friends. Put simply, Liselle helps several Kelles fulfill their Manuel Ferrara fantasies, all while creating some pretty amazing content.

Liselle begins each match with a lighthearted but in-depth interview, plumbing the depths of her friends' psyches in order to identify their respective Manuels—who they would just love to work with but haven't so far. She then changes the subject to business matters and asks the friend to work in a scene with some other partner. Everyone agrees to the terms of this standard casting procedure.

But Liselle is crafty. After everything is apparently set, she goes out and secretly books her friends' respective Manuels for the upcoming scenes. When the shoots finally take place, the lucky friends show up for a regular day's work and . . . surprise! They learn at the last minute that it's their Manuel (who's also in on the plot) they'll be working with. And my goodness, the sparks fly!

What we end up with in *Match Mates* are five scenes that are fantastic—hot, lusty, and a little bit giddy. (You'd be excited if you got to work with your dream lover, too. Don't act like you don't have one.) Liselle shoots much of the close-up action herself, but there's a second, more distant camera that captures her working with the performers. It's voyeurism squared, original and fresh, absolutely creative, and extremely thought provoking.

That's because adult performers have unfulfilled desires too, just like Kelle had for the real Manuel. And when an unexpected opportunity to turn those fantasies into reality presents itself, well, it's exciting. The performers in *Match Mates* and Kelle's giddy desire point to a very human truth: Porn stars have fantasies, just like the rest of us.

But back to Kelle. Though things got extremely difficult for her for a while, these days she's doing really well. She's moved on to new career opportunities within the adult industry, and she's planning her wedding to a guy who, in my opinion, is much better suited for her than her ex. Her work and her life are almost entirely behind the scenes now, while her significance in the adult industry community has increased dramatically. She's become a leader. We don't talk as much anymore, but she seems really happy.

It's interesting to think about Kelle and the path her life has taken during the time I've known her. When we first met, she seemed to have everything she'd ever dreamed of. As it turns out though, Kelle wanted so much more, and everything that seemed so set in her life was simply a transitional stage in her overall process. Chances are, she's already going through another. Pretty soon, she'll again be different than she is today. We all will.

16

The Real Linda Lovelace
(née Boreman, née Marchiano)

MANY YEARS AGO, I BELIEVED THE INTRO TO WOMEN'S Studies–type hype about "The Real Linda Lovelace" and Gloria Steinem's tragic recounting of a life leveled by pornography.[1] But since then, when I actually did some research of my own, I have developed a more nuanced understanding of a life leveled by severe physical, sexual, and emotional spousal abuse. Nevertheless, we still hear that story about Linda—that porn was what set her life spiraling out of control. And it simply isn't true.

Linda Susan Boreman was born in New York on January 10, 1949. In 1969, she was recuperating from a near-fatal car accident when she met Chuck Traynor. They married soon after, and Chuck very quickly became Linda's "suitcase pimp"—a derisive term for a husband-boyfriend-lover who tries to garner prestige by pimping his lady's wares and skills. Chuck was also a brutally aggressive man who subjected Linda to years of violent sexual servitude. This included forced prostitution and performance in an array of short independent underground loops, things with titles like *Dogarama* (aka *Dog Fucker*) and *Piss Orgy*. Trust me: These titles are exactly what you think they are.

Now, back in those days, there was no formal business focused on adult content production. What we have today—a global, professional adult entertainment industry—didn't begin to emerge in the US until the 1980s. The seeds of a formal industry had already been sown by the early seventies, however, and a handful of independent producers were right on the brink, thinking they were about to make it big time with porn. True to form, Chuck was there in the mix, prepping Linda for the payday he just knew was coming.

Enter *Deep Throat*.

Gerard Damiano's *Deep Throat*, released in 1972, was the first-ever adult feature film "talkie." Plot-wise, it's absolutely ridiculous—a tragic tale of sexual dissatisfaction. You see, the young woman lead has been doing a whole lot of fucking, but she's still dissatisfied with sex. She wants to feel dams bursting and bells ringing, but those things just aren't happening. Eventually, she takes her problem to a local physician, who finds that her clitoris is not where it's supposed to be. In fact, quite mysteriously, that little bugger is actually located in her throat, so, oh my goodness, it's no wonder vaginal penetration isn't doing it for you, honey! The doctor cleverly prescribes deep-throating as much cock as possible (including his) because, you know, that's how she gets off. So our lead, now brimming with possibility, goes around doing just that. Occasionally she's dressed as a nurse. At one point, she shaves her pussy.

It all makes perfect sense. (Not really.)

Linda, who had long since perfected the sword-swallowing trick required to play this demanding role, was cast. Truth be told, much of the script was probably written with her specific capabilities in mind.

And in an attempt to both elevate and exoticise her plainly beautiful girl-next-door shtick, Chuck and company dubbed her "Linda Lovelace." Interestingly, in the film's opening credits, Linda is billed as playing "herself."

I always thought this was noteworthy, this idea of Linda playing "herself" in *Deep Throat*. She was already playing a character, one not necessarily of her own design, in embodying Linda Lovelace. But the Linda Lovelace character's allure relied upon at least two characteristics that actually belonged to the real Linda—her uncommon sexual acrobatic abilities and her girl-next-door looks. Consequently, what we ended up with in *Deep Throat* was a character who was presented as "real" and was reliant upon actual physical skill, all while being impossibly contrived. This was a sleight-of-hand that conflated fantasy and reality in a way that was relatively uncommon, at least back in those days. I always wondered what impact this had, both on society in the early seventies and on gender and sexualities and beyond.

I digress.

Deep Throat's popularity skyrocketed, and it's been estimated that ticket sales rivaled those of Francis Ford Coppola's *The Godfather*, which was released the same year. Linda quickly became the face of "porno chic," the cultural phenomenon of porn being acceptable and cool. Films like *Behind the Green Door, The Devil in Miss Jones,* and *Deep Throat* were discussed publicly by celebrities and taken seriously by film critics. Everyone wanted a piece of Linda, and, for a very brief moment, she was *it*.

But Linda's life wasn't just fun and games and cocksucking. Chuck was still around. And all during the filming of *Deep Throat*, for years before, and for almost a year after, Linda was being severely abused by him. It didn't stop when the crew was in the next room, nor did it abate as she became the face of the new pornographic age. In fact, given what experts tell us about patterns of abuse, I imagine Chuck's aggressions became even more intense as Linda became more and more famous.

Eventually, though, Linda had enough. She managed to escape Chuck in 1973 and went into hiding for several months. When she emerged, it was with the hopes of cultivating a mainstream film career, but she was offered very little work, none of it very artistic or substantial, and all requiring some degree of simulated sex or nudity. Linda refused most of these roles.

Broke, stigmatized, and now struggling with legal troubles too, Linda eventually married her childhood friend Larry Marchiano. They attempted to set up a quiet life together. (This, incidentally, is roughly where the 2013 biopic *Lovelace* cuts off.) But times were tough. In what I imagine was an attempt to dig herself out of a financial hole and achieve some measure of catharsis, Linda published an account of her life as Linda Lovelace, *Ordeal*, in 1980.[2] The book got quite a bit of attention, resulting in a promotional appearance on *The Phil Donahue Show* (a big deal back in those days). This event facilitated Linda's connection with Gloria Steinem and an emerging legion of anti-porn activists.

Many gender-related social changes were taking shape at that time, and while Linda was working to rebuild her life during the mid-to-late-seventies, many feminist activists and scholars were critiquing what they found to be sexist and violent imagery in US culture and media. This included the imagery found in adult content. These critiques came in many forms, including work by the activist/protest collective Women Against Pornography (WAP), which was formed in New York in 1979. Linda, now Linda Marchiano, became a prominent spokesperson for the organization through one of WAP's most strident supporters, Gloria Steinem.

When anti-porn activists and scholars developed a city ordinance demanding all "pornographic material" (which was never clearly defined) be outlawed from Minneapolis, Minnesota, in 1983, members of Women Against Pornography, including Linda, testified on its behalf. Much of her testimony during the Minneapolis Proceedings would reappear in 1985's Meese Commission report.

You see, fifteen years earlier, in 1970, the Presidential Commission on Pornography's findings had stated that there was no discernible link between sexually explicit material and criminal and/or violent behavior. In other words, experts could find no links between porn and violence. But in 1985, President Ronald Reagan felt it necessary to give then–Attorney General Edwin Meese one year and half a million dollars to determine the "real" effects of porn in the US. (Because the Presidential Commission on Pornography's findings weren't real enough, I guess.) That circus would come to be known as the Meese Commission.

Many notable people were involved, but the clear star witness in the Meese Commission process was the now-repentant former starlet of the new pornographic age, Linda Lovelace. She had become a vehement anti-porn activist, which was not surprising, in my opinion. Her brains were probably so scrambled from the abuse she endured at the hands of Chuck Traynor that she needed some kind of outlet, some place to channel her energy and emotions. And her graphic and tragic account of a life *supposedly* leveled by pornography provided anti-porn activists a flesh-and-bone example of how destructive adult content and its production *supposedly* were. Perfect! Well, not exactly.

But why not? Linda had obviously been involved in porn production, and she certainly had a story to tell.

In any situation, reliance on one example is perilous at best. And reliance on *this* one example in *this* particular situation was particularly perilous for at least two reasons. First, by her own account, Linda was in no way abused or coerced by porn producers. That was the work solely of Chuck Traynor. Second, Linda's accounts speak to her experiences alone. Even if she had been abused or coerced by early pornographers (which she, in her own words, had not been), one person's story cannot be used to characterize everyone's experiences and/or the qualities found in an entire segment of society.

You might think that activists and scholars would be aware of the dangers associated with this sort of overgeneralizing. You might also think that activists and scholars would refrain from exploiting a survivor's experiences. But apparently, at least in this case, you'd be wrong.

The use of Linda's life story by anti-porn activists as an exemplar during the Meese Commission was inappropriate, overbroad, manipulative, and exploitative. It's sad to consider the degree to which these crusaders—feminists and activists and scholars and conservatives alike—attempted to capitalize on the celebrity and tragedy of "Linda Lovelace," all to further their respective causes.

And don't be fooled! This kind of use and abuse happens to this day. Anti-porn activists repeatedly exploit, and in some cases fabricate, former porn performers' and/or survivors' experiences, all to achieve their own ends.

Then the 1980s came to a close, and Linda disappeared from the public eye altogether.

Linda Boreman died in the Denver Health Medical Center on April 22, 2002, from injuries she suffered in a car accident on April 3 of that same year. By all accounts, her life was so sad.

But then again, who am I to judge? Linda had two kids and twenty-two years of marriage with Larry before they divorced in 1996; she got to go to the Oscars, which is something most people never get to do; and, for better or worse, she did have an amazing physical ability that many have tried to emulate. Though I certainly feel it necessary to call attention to the gender and sexuality inequality issues that may somehow compel a person to swallow an entire penis, the fact remains that the lady had skills.

So I don't really know about Linda. I wonder about many of her choices. How much of her life was a product of insurmountable manipulations that undoubtedly impacted every single "choice" she made? How did these manipulations shape her legacy? And how much of her story is actually hers?

There's a lot of sadness associated with Linda—sadness and anger and loss. Regardless of all that, though, I think the most important thing to remember is that Linda lived. She lived, she helped shape our culture, and she was a survivor.

17

Sexuality Through the Ages

THE FIRST TIME I SAW BONNIE ROTTEN WAS THE SAME time most people first saw her—featured in her very own star showcase in 2012, Digital Sin's *Meet Bonnie Rotten*.[1] That was her catapult.

Bonnie did a handful of scenes in 2012, but 2013 was her year. She blew up the porn world in tough-girl features and super-hard hardcore. She was sweet and vivacious and easy to work with. She had cute little freckles, a rockin' new rack, and was already mostly covered in tattoos (unusual on such a popular performer, even today). In January 2014, Bonnie was named AVN's Female Performer of the Year, which is essentially the highest honor anyone in the adult industry can get.

But when I first "met" Bonnie, by proxy of watching *Meet Bonnie*, I felt like an asshole—an ageist asshole. Her film was beautifully done by some of the best in the business. Her scenes were diverse and hot, though a little coltish at times. (The job was still new to her, so I gave her a break.) But in spite of Bonnie's solid sex performances and the film's technical and aesthetic merits, I still didn't like it. I didn't like it because, when Bonnie spoke to the camera, she seemed like a kid. It was creepy. Way creepy. I was actually so troubled by *Meet Bonnie* that I didn't feel I could write the film a fair review. How do you discuss something that's good but that simultaneously makes you feel uncomfortable *in a bad way?*

— x x x —

Let me tell you a not-so-secret secret: "Young girl" porn really freaks me out. And I'm not talking about the campus coeds (*wink, wink*) content or the stuff where an obviously adult woman is costumed in knee socks and a pleated skirt. What I'm talking about is the "barely legal," "really tight teenage" stuff. Call me kooky, but something about a braceface young lady flashing her ID to prove her eighteenth birthday was yesterday rattles me to my core. I say this knowing several things.

First, young people have sexualities and experience sexual desire; thus, eighteen-year-olds have sexualities and experience sexual desire. Who am I to judge how they express it, and who am I to judge those who desire it? Second, legal age really is an arbitrary assignment based on culture and era. Consequently, in another part of the world or two hundred years ago, those aforementioned tight teenagers may've been well into cougarhood. Third, this type of content provides an outlet for people who have certain predilections and issues generally frowned upon by society. Think about it: Isn't it better for those on the hunt for youth to indulge in a professional production featuring a legal adult than to go out looking for teenagers on their own? (I think you know what I'm getting at here.) And finally, there are all sorts of media that focus on youth—music and modeling and savvy young genius upstarts. We as a culture love it if it's fresh. Why should our sexy time predilections be any different?

I recently wrote something regarding age-centered content as it occurs in porn production and consumption for the academic journal *Porn Studies*:

> The illusion of youth has been a significant theme in adult content since the 1970s, and it continues to be extremely popular today. Young girl—or "teen"—content is a genre of porn that focuses on young-looking women performers. Youth is conveyed via costuming and by the actual age of the performers themselves—women who typically work in this genre are of-age teens (eighteen and nineteen years of age) or are in their early twenties.[2]

But when I wrote this passage I forgot to emphasize that, though women who typically work in this genre are of-age teens or are in their early twenties, they are occasionally older than their early twenties and never are they younger than eighteen. At least, not in professional adult content production they aren't. You see, if there's something that creeps me out even more than the legal representation of teenagers in porn, it's graphic media depictions of child sexual abuse—what's commonly referred to as "child pornography" or "CP." I put these phrases in quotes, and I generally refuse to even write or say them, for one primary reason: They don't exist.

Now, let me restate that last part in another way. Graphic media depictions of child sexual abuse both exist and are highly illegal in the United States. Pornography, on the other hand, is a legal enterprise, made for and featuring consenting adults. Professionally produced adult content made in the US does not feature models or performers who are under the age of eighteen. The phrases "CP" and "child pornography" thus connect the sexual abuse of minors (illegal) with porn production in the US (legal) in an extremely inappropriate and problematic way.

How do I know this? Well, not one rigorous academic study or criminal case has identified a connection between professional pornographers and graphic media depictions of child sexual abuse. Further, porn is currently being made in the US, at this very moment. Don't you think adult content producers would be locked away for life instead of paying taxes and filing film permits if they were abusing minors?

Regardless, the exploitation and abuse of minors is nasty, and our obsession with youth is pervasive. And in porn, this obsession doesn't only come through a heterosexual gaze eyeballing young women. "Twink" (slang for a youthful looking man) content, for example, emphasizes young-looking men performers working with other young men, satisfying a big demand in the gay market. Age-centered themes are also prevalent in lesbian content, with commonplace emphases on both young women performers and the sub-genre of older-younger women couplings. And even now, at this very moment, porn producers are scouring the earth for sexy young studs to satisfy the increasingly demanding heterosexual woman consumer—because that soccer mom down your block loves looking at some hot washboard twenty-year-old abs. And so does her daughter.

Another interesting thing about age in porn is how compressed it is. Twenty-six-year-olds are MILFs, and any woman over thirty is a cougar. And I guess if we're filtering our sexual gaze through the eyes of youth, which is something we love to do in all aspects of social life, then this perspective doesn't seem all that off base. But it does skew the "look"—the perspective shaping our collective gaze—that we have of grown women, especially in porn. Women are inevitably corralled into some version of motherhood, or they're cast as sexed-up vixens preoccupied with draining all the lifeblood they can from any available source. Our tendency to put women into one of two problematic boxes is almost as off-putting to me as those tight teens I was talking about before.

Times change, though, and content evolves. And occasionally, we do get different representations of womanhood and, interestingly, women's interpersonal relationships. Consider, for example, Wicked Pictures' *Divorcees*, a laugh-out-loud hilarious, wistful, and empowering exploration of women's friendships, which is also porn. Written and directed by Stormy Daniels, this film—which is occasionally painfully on point in its real-life ludicrousness—is a thoughtful coming-of-age story about grown women. Here's the synopsis from the box copy:

> Now in their thirties, best friends Leanne (Stormy Daniels), Stacy (Julia Ann) and Carmen (Veronica Avluv) find themselves single and somewhat emotionally lost. After trying to heal through traditional methods, the trio decides a road trip is in order. Comedy— and Hot Sex—ensues as each tries drastically different approaches to get back in the saddle!

So three BFFs in their thirties are all single. They're all also pretty quirky. Stacy is a little surly and 100 percent over sex, relationships, and guys in general; freshly cheated upon, Leanne is a bit more rageful and raw beneath her calm exterior; and Carmen is having a relationship with a fitness instructor (via her television) and her vibrator. She's really a mess.

After some seriously funny and occasionally bittersweet sequences in which each lady tries various tactics to reclaim her mojo, they decide to go on a trip to LA, where everyone calls them ma'am. And they score some drugs! And Carmen stalks Ricardo (the fitness instructor) with a star map. And Leanne and Stacy meet DJ Deejay and his pal Clooney. Good-natured shenanigans ensue, and fun is had by all. Sounds cute, right? But there's so much more.

Divorcees is good because it's well done. The plot is simple but entertaining, the production value is high, and the sex is steamy. But *Divorcees* is also good because it explores many greater dimensions and themes, all of them relevant to real life. In other words, this film is good because it's exceptional.

It's worth noting that Carmen is not a divorcée—she's a widow. Though this is only touched upon for a moment, it's rare for adult films to reflect such a true-to-life experience. *Divorcees* looks at progressive ways of dealing with events and scenarios that can actually happen. As sad as it may be, relationships often end. People die, people cheat, and people grow in different directions. But what happens after? Seriously, what happens to "normal" people after their lives change? *Divorcees* explores the ridiculous and the mundane, all without some trite thirty-plus fountain-of-youth fantasy story line.

This film also shows women as friends. Now, maybe it's just me, but over and over and *over* again you see media representations of women in competition, women backstabbing, and women just hating other women. But *Divorcees* doesn't do that. *Divorcees* is about three ladies who may tease each other and who may all be very different, but they don't hate each other. In fact, the primary motivation for the entire plot is care and concern for one another's well-being. It was refreshing, both in terms of shattering stereotypes and (I'd like to think) showing a more nuanced version of reality.

Finally, *Divorcees* shows grown women as desirable and desiring, all while not being pigeonholed as cougars or MILFs. Now, there's absolutely nothing wrong with cougars and MILFs, nor is there anything wrong with presenting young(er) ladies as desirable, but it was nice to see three beautiful mature women being showcased without all those extraneous tropes and stereotypes.

This movie was about friendships and loss and moving on. It was a coming-of-age story for an age bracket that's often dismissed and rarely discussed, at least not without derision. It was about life moving forward and being a fun, silly, and unexpected adventure. It was women-centered and progressive. It made me think.

Our consideration of adult content is shaped by many things, including space and place, era, and cultural trends. Currently, we are led to look at young adulthood and youth as both desirable and problematic, a stage of life in which people are simultaneously autonomous and not, sexual and not. We have drawn a series of somewhat arbitrary lines around a collection of statuses common to this stage of life that end up shaping how we view the world. Thus, young girl content freaks me out, but also it pisses me off every time I see one of those wildly inaccurate descriptors I mentioned earlier. And I get all teary when I see something that shows women over the age of thirty as multifaceted and stimulating. Maybe this is because I'm well over thirty myself.

There's room in the human experience for all of it, for desire at all ages (just as long as consent is involved and kids are not). And even though some of it may make us uncomfortable at various stages in our lives, we have to allow for sexual expression at all points. And we must also allow that expression to evolve.

Since I "met" her in 2012, I've seen Bonnie Rotten in many different scenes and roles. I've read her interviews, seen her speak to the press, and heard quite a few behind-the-scenes stories. And I've never since gotten that same "young" feeling from her. Years have passed, and her reputation remains flawless. (Killer businesswoman is now regularly included in her inventory of accolades.) In many ways, she's stepping into shoes once filled by Stormy Daniels, who rode a similar rocket ship when she was similarly young. I look forward to seeing how Bonnie evolves. I will work to be mindful of my own evolutions throughout that process.

18

The Real Traci Elizabeth Lords

WE ALL HAVE OUR HOT-BUTTON ISSUES, THOSE THINGS people can push that end up pushing us right over the edge. And, as we know, one of my most sensitive buttons is related to the misnomer "child pornography." Now, as I've said before, the sexual exploitation and abuse of underage persons happens. It happens all too often, and occasionally people even record and attempt to distribute it. In every instance, this type of abuse is horrifying and extremely problematic, but calling instances of recorded child sexual abuse "child pornography" is also problematic. It muddies the waters and conflates a wealth of issues, including the fact that the professional adult content production industry in the United States does not and has never *knowingly* produced content featuring an underage person. Unfortunately however, this does not mean that an underage person has never been featured in it.

—— x x x ——

Nora Kuzma was born on May 7, 1968. According to her autobiography, *Underneath It All*, she had a pretty difficult time growing up.

Between her parents' volatile relationship, which eventually ended in divorce, lots of moving around from the Midwest to Florida to Southern California, being sexually assaulted by a sixteen-year-old when she was ten, and her mom's creepy, lecherous hippie boyfriend hanging around, Nora was already walking a perilous line by the time she reached junior high.

Stealing, smoking pot, drinking, and having sex with her seventeen-year-old boyfriend all amounted to Nora's getting pregnant at age fifteen. And with the baby daddy refusing to get involved and her mother off somewhere, she turned to the only adult she knew for help—Roger, the aforementioned creepy hippie lecher. An abortion became just another event on the long list of things this young girl had to endure.

But Nora was a survivor, and, as she became increasingly self-reliant (that is, neglected and unsupervised), she began to realize that one thing you need to survive in this life is money. Nora needed a job, but she quickly found that there weren't too many well-paying opportunities available for those in her age bracket. So with a borrowed birth certificate and a subsequently acquired legal California ID "proving" she was twenty-two-year-old Kristie Nussman, Nora found herself at an audition for "figure modeling" (legitimately, bikini, fitness, or nude modeling for things like art classes; illegitimately, a sneaky way to get doe-eyed young women to take their tops off) at Jim South's World Modeling. Roger, ever helpful, gave her a ride to Porn Valley.

Just like that, in the blink of eye, Nora became Kristie, and Kristie started going by Traci Lords. And since she was still only fifteen, Roger became her chauffeur. Traci was wildly popular and photographed in countless pages of print porn. Eventually, though, her images saturated that media, and the work began to dry up. The only difference was that now Nora was even more desperate for cash.

You see, in order to psych herself up for all of that naked figure modeling, Nora had allegedly acquired a sizable coke habit, which she was topping off with a bit of a drinking problem. And though multiple industry insiders around her during these times report having never seen her use drugs on even one occasion, the need to manage her habit is what reportedly prompted her to make the jump from nude modeling to hardcore. The rest is history.

By the end of 1984, at the age of sixteen, Traci had morphed into one of the most recognized and sought-after women performers in the adult industry. Over the course of roughly the next year and a half, she would star in more than seventy adult films. And in only one of those films, *Traci, I Love You*, was she over eighteen.

Traci's true identity and age were revealed in May 1986, just days after her eighteenth birthday. According to her autobiography, which she wrote under her eventually legally adopted name, Traci Elizabeth Lords, authorities had been aware of her case for three years—essentially, for the entire time she'd been working in adult entertainment. Industry insiders reported being shown during questioning photographic documentation (stakeout footage taken from afar) of Traci's earliest work. Allegedly, law enforcement was gathering information for something having to do with the Meese Commission, watching underage Nora fuck and be fucked all the while.

Though authorities apparently were long aware of Traci's deception, members of the industry reportedly were not. Upon learning her true age and identity, many people said they felt extremely guilty and foolish. How had they not put two and two together? A Polaroid photo serendipitously snapped by prolific industry photographer Suze Randall, showing Traci with her legal California-issued Kristie Nussman ID, was one of the only things that prevented the industry's immediate and total shutdown in 1986.

And then there was all the content that had to be destroyed. Regardless of the industry's misinformation about her age, countless units of Traci's films had to be pulled from producers' warehouses and destroyed. The loss of this stock and revenue alone was enough to put some companies out of business, and most immediately ceased any dealings in Traci's products, which were literally child pornography.

Perhaps looking to minimize their years of data gathering, undercover investigators were able to find one person—Rubin "Ruby" Gottesman of X-Citement Video—who had learned of Traci's true age and was still willing to sell her films. In 1987, Gottesman was convicted of knowingly trafficking sexual content featuring an underage person. His conviction was appealed on the grounds of vague and overbroad wording in the Protection of Children Against Sexual Exploitation Act of 1977 (US Code, Title 18, Section 2251–2253); however, the original conviction was upheld by the *United States v. X-Citement Video* decision (513 US 64; 1994). With the exception of Gottesman, not one member of the adult industry was convicted of producing, possessing, or trafficking "child pornography" in light of the Kuzma/Lords case—probably because they had all been scammed.

A similar scam happened again, years later, this time with Alexandra Quinn. Like Traci, Alexandra misrepresented her age with falsified legal identification, in this case, a Canadian passport. And like Traci's films, Alexandra's were destroyed immediately. But, unlike Traci, Alexandra eventually went back into the business when she was of age.

Although the Nora Kuzma/Traci Lords "child pornography" case was not used as evidence in the Meese Commission, her story and Linda Lovelace's were invoked regularly in anti-pornography activism during the late 1980s. Both were used as "evidence" that women are systematically tortured and physically abused and children are sexually exploited through the course of porn production. But these instances actually exemplify why conservative and feminist work done in opposition of the industry during the 1980s failed to shut down or even limit porn production: Women were not being systematically abused by the industry, and the industry was not exploiting children.

Although unquestionably tragic, both Linda's and Traci's cases point to the wider social problems of partner and child abuse, child neglect, and interpersonal manipulation. These issues are not the "fault" of the adult industry, nor are they its sole responsibility to repair. Regardless though, just like Linda Lovelace, the name Traci Lords is still tossed around by anti-porn activists, scholars, and commentators—folks who generally don't have a clear understanding of the facts.

Since her infamous adolescence, Traci Lords has done all right for herself. She has been in several mainstream movies, including John Waters' *Cry-Baby*, Stephen Norrington's *Blade*, and Kevin Smith's ridiculous *Zack and Miri Make a Porno*. She's done lots of TV, including multiple episodes of *Melrose Place* and *Roseanne* in the mid-nineties and nineteen episodes of *Profiler* soon after. She even released a techno-ish album called *1000 Fires* in 1995, which I absolutely loved when I was in college.

Traci Lords has gone from being *Two Timing Traci* to a solid B-level actress doing a helluva lot more with her career in front of the camera than most people who desperately seek that sort of thing. She is incredibly beautiful, is a mom, and wrote a very compelling account of her life thus far.

Traci is also a survivor of reprehensible parenting and neglect. (Incidentally, why was Roger never sent to jail? That boggles my mind. And what about the California DMV? What about the role their negligence played in all of this?) I honestly cannot imagine the strength and tenacity it must have taken to move beyond the stigma she's certainly felt to cultivate the life and livelihood she has. And because we as a culture are so hypocritical and judgmental, she likely still has to deal with her porn star past in some capacity every single day. Even now, thirty-odd years later.

And yet, I still feel rather ambivalent about her.

In my opinion, a child cannot be held accountable for decisions in the same way that an adult should, especially if there is a parent figure or a grown-up encouraging the exceptionally poor ones. At the same time, to assume that kids are too stupid or incapable of understanding the consequences of their actions in adolescence, even just a little . . . well, that's just ridiculous.

I don't necessarily think Traci "blames" the porn community for her stint in the industry. By her own account, she knew what she was doing, and she knew it was a less-than-good idea. (Or was it? Where would her career be today without the fuel of her infamy?) I wonder, though, if she blames herself. Was it her fault? Totally? Partially? Is fault even relevant at this point?

In my view, Traci's story stopped being about her a long time ago, but I think the people whose lives she touched probably still think about her often. Because the saddest and most commonly overlooked part of this tale has to do with the industry insiders Traci impacted. Think about it: How would you feel if you were a performer who had essentially been tricked into having sex with an underage person? Or if you were a director who had filmed it? And what about the producers and distributors, the business people who suffered severe financial loss and, in many cases, devastation? Traci cost a lot of working people and small-business owners their livelihoods. And some of these folks are still there, working in porn and shaking their heads about a system that allowed a teenager to take everything.

I wonder, where is the book about them?

19

Stripper Dildo Lollipop Party

A GIRLFRIEND OF MINE GOT MARRIED RECENTLY, AND, leading up to the nuptials, my friends and I wanted to celebrate with every kind of festivity imaginable. Unfortunately though, due to various extenuating circumstances, a stripper dildo lollipop party wasn't going to happen. Instead, we went all out for Cindy's bridal shower, an extravagant weekend brunch at the fanciest of fancy LA-area hotels. It was an international, tri-generational event (four generations, actually, if you counted one of us having a three-month case of the babies), with attendees coming all the way from China and Germany.

Everyone was super dolled up, even me. I had taken great pains to branch out from my everyday attire (yoga pants, Converse, and one of an endless array of ratty band t-shirts), arriving instead in a day dress and matching sun hat. This whole look was complemented with a lavender spring bag and a mid-size box wrapped in silver matte paper, topped with a voluminous bow. I looked like a duchess (and a stranger). Perfect.

But what was inside that box? All the ladies, but not the grandmothers, were nervous. Because it was me, everyone suspected that I wouldn't have been able to resist inserting a little raunch into Cindy's very ladylike affair. So, *what was inside that box?*

Rewind to earlier in the week, when I had walked to my neighborhood sex shop. I'd never been inside before, but it was a seemingly subdued store located squarely in the middle of a relatively fancy touristy shopping boulevard. Now, I've been to a hefty handful of sex shops in my life, brick-and-mortar storefronts that run the gamut: from the larger-than-life Hustler Hollywood store on Sunset Boulevard to the quirkiest little retro place in St. Pete Beach, from high-end Dallas-area boutiques to highway-adjacent neon emporiums that are literally sticky. I've seen enough of them to guesstimate a store's target market pretty accurately. Given the surroundings, I was hoping that my neighborhood sex shop would have something appropriately tasteful for the bride-to-be.

And what a bride-to-be she was. Cindy is an interesting mix of brassy bold and austere. She runs one-third of a successful multinational corporation and travels extensively in the name of her passions for food and yoga. Not surprisingly, she's open to every new person and every new experience. But she can also be a little particular.

So contrary to everyone's expectations and fears, when I went in search of a gift, I wasn't looking for a box of cock-tail straws or bulk pricing on fifteen Clone-A-Willy kits. Really, why poke the bear? It was Cindy's special girls' day, and I didn't think she would appreciate such nonsense. What I was looking for was something a little fun and sexy but also classy—some subtle raunch à la Agent Provocateur meets Trashy Lingerie. Or maybe something stimulating in a therapeutic, organic kind of way. I thought this order, albeit tall, would be a bit of a no-brainer at my neighborhood sex shop. As I said, it was right in the middle of a very prominent, well-trafficked shopping area amid decently high-end stores.

But the more I thought about it, the more I started pondering a gift certificate. Because I wasn't actually going to pick out a toy for her. We're close, but not that close! And besides, shopping for something sexy for the bedroom might be a fun adventure for her and her soon-to-be-spouse. I envisioned a personalized gift basket comprised of a chic embossed certificate surrounded by some sexy soy candles, sensation-based lubes, and pheromone-infused massage oils, maybe with an elegant feather tickler as garnish—a beautiful collection of free-form erotic adventure!

But it was not to be. I knew that as soon as I stepped through the shop's door.

Putting it kindly, the store was definitely on the seedier end of the sex toy store spectrum. Less kindly, the entire place was a disaster. It was dirty and disorganized. The walls were jam-packed with product, but the store still felt empty because of the underutilized floor space in the middle. And in a particularly genius move, higher-end products were adjacent to harder toys. Imagine the Lelo products right next to the Fuck Me Silly Mega Masturbators. (Look 'em up!) And the DVD selection—the one in the basement and lit by buzzing neon lights? Creepy and depressing!

Now, I'm no marketing feng shui display expert. I know little to nothing about harmonizing the human shopping experience with its environment. I also don't know anything about running a brick-and-mortar store of any kind; aside from a summer stint organizing the Girls and Shoes departments at Target when I was eighteen, I've never worked at anything even remotely retail. But I'm a pretty experienced consumer, I'm fairly well versed in sex-related products, and as I've said, I've been inside many sex shops.

And I was shocked by this store! Specifically, I was shocked by how uncomfortable I felt inside it. Especially given its surroundings.

I couldn't imagine a setup that would be less conducive to enticing the shoppers milling about on the streets outside. I couldn't imagine a person popping in for some lube after a fancy lunch and some retail therapy. Well, actually I could imagine it. I just couldn't imagine it happening at this store. And I couldn't imagine my friend having an enjoyable experience with her partner in this place. The Hustler store perhaps, but not here.

Maybe I was wrong. My neighborhood sex shop was in business, so obviously everyone was not as put off, but the entire experience both depressed and floored me. I wanted to support adult novelty retail and my local economy, but this place had nothing to offer me, not even for the stripper dildo lollipop party we weren't having.

This entire sequence of events illustrated a wealth of lessons, both about the challenges one might face when attempting to "go local" by patronizing smaller, independent businesses and about the disconnects that can occur between an old-school business and an emerging clientele. In the end, Cindy got a typical gift card from a typical chain store, one that specialized in kitchen gadgets and home goods. That's what was inside that perfect mid-size box wrapped in silver matte paper and topped with a voluminous bow. And I got a lesson in DIY gift baskets and online shopping—namely, start early, or you'll be out of luck. Bummer.

20

Coming Out Porno

FOR A LONG TIME, I LIVED A DOUBLE LIFE.

For years, I worked quietly as a graduate student and professor. This, in and of itself, was difficult. Teaching four courses at a pair of very different schools—one elite liberal arts university and one community college—often made me feel a bit unhinged. The students' needs and each institution's expectations couldn't have been more different. At one school, I had parents confronting me about the B their third-year student earned in my upper-level Identities course (no joke); at the other, I had a young single mother in hysterics when her babysitter flaked at the end of the semester. To this day, the only time I've ever done child-care work was while one of my students was completing her final exam. Top that with the tedium required to complete a dissertation, and you get a pretty clear picture of me in my early thirties.

But the difficulties I experienced while balancing what were essentially two (maybe three) full-time jobs were just the tip of the iceberg. The weighty remainder of my double life existed just beneath the surface. Because even though I had completed the fieldwork portion of my dissertation by 2008 and technically needed nothing more, I was still very much involved with the adult industry.

Given my roots in feminist scholarship and social justice, I felt compelled to give back to the community that had contributed so significantly to my work. So, as I pecked away at my dissertation and dealt with various student meltdowns and successes, I also continued helping out at conventions and the like, contributing wherever I felt ethically comfortable. And as more and more time passed, I started to see additional holes in the public's understanding of porn. I witnessed blatant, outlandish bias in the mainstream media, and I cringed as other academics made endless off-base and problematic statements about the adult business and the humans (currently or formerly) involved therein. And it came from all sides, at any given moment.

For example, I was out with a group of people for a close friend's birthday. Patrick had a large and diverse collection of associates from a variety of backgrounds, including one rather unsavory woman in "feminist media studies" (her words). I had never met her, but she was very curious about me.

"So, Pat tells me you do some interesting stuff," she fished. "Like, with porno?"

"Kind of," I said, already apprehensive about where this was going. "I study social movements in the absence of on-the-ground organizing and activism. The adult entertainment industry is the case I'm looking at."

She took a second to process, then dived right in: "So, you've gone to all those shows in Vegas and stuff, right?" I nodded, and she continued, now louder, addressing the rest of the group: "God, we should all go and watch the porn people and laugh at them!"

"Laugh at 'them'?" I asked. "Do you mean laugh at the people working, or do you mean laugh at the people who go to the show? Or everyone? We could laugh at all 'those' people. Maybe that would be fun?" I suggested, laying the sarcasm on thick.

"God, yes!" she squealed. "What a bunch of freaks!"

"Freaks" worthy only of mockery—this was the unfiltered response from a person who described her work as "feminist media studies." I politely excused myself.

By the time I graduated, PhD in hand despite all odds, I was ready to rip my hair out. I had been maintaining my public composure about porn for years by that point, but I just couldn't do it any longer. As I've mentioned, academic publishing takes a long time, and I wanted to find a way to get information out into the world more quickly and in a more accessible way. So even though I was absolutely terrified to do so, I started a blog upon completion of my degree. PVVOnline .com is "critical commentary on adult production"—interviews, film and content reviews, and my perspective on porn as a sociologically significant dimension of our wider culture. It was my coming out as a sociologist and as someone who was interested in the adult entertainment industry.

Around that same time, I also began working on more in-the-trenches, community-oriented research and scholarship. In the fall of 2010, mere months after I had collected my degree, I conducted a series of focus groups and interviews with adult performers working in the Los Angeles and San Francisco Bay areas. A lot of political things had been going on in porn, developments related to health, law, and free speech.

One major issue had to do with workplace safety on set, or what's come to be known as the condom debate: Should performers be required to wear condoms during vaginal and anal penetrative sex scenes? Though there's more to this conversation, there were two distinct sides to the argument. On one hand, you had the adult industry raising free-speech concerns, bodily autonomy issues, and their STI-infection-mitigation-via-standardized-testing protocol. On the other hand, you had safer-sex rhetoric, the big business of sexual health, and the fact that people often misappropriate adult content for sex education. In the middle of all this were the performers, the folks who were actually impacted on every level. I was curious as to what performers actually thought about the issues, so I designed a study and set about asking them.

Prior to this cycle of data gathering, I had only been a fly on the wall—an ethnographer, an observer, a voyeur. And though I'd certainly done my fair share of informal, conversational interviews, this was the first time I had ever sat down, on purpose, with currently working (and in some cases, really prominent) adult performers in order to ask them structured, point-blank questions. Structured, point-blank, loaded questions. So in order to be effective and respectful, I had to learn to speak Porn Star Porno. (Yes, it's a dialect.)

Like any subculture or group, porn performers have their own way of saying certain things. Porn Star Porno involves a vernacular drenched in bodily fluids and sexual acrobatics and consists of all sorts of things that those outside the industry don't really understand, much less say in polite conversation. So even though I was perfectly comfortable saying "vagina" to a room full of twentysomethings taking a Gender and Sexualities course, saying "pussy" in lieu of "vagina" to a small group of slightly fussy porn performers made me sweat, just a little. So did saying "cock," "blowbang," "cum fart,"[1] and any number of other things.

But I got it done.

These interviews ended up giving rise to a really great study that I published in *Stanford Law and Policy Review*.[2] More important, this allowed me to take another step into the adult community. I could feel people relax a bit more around me because my words and my writing conveyed that I was both interested in and familiar with their work.

As I continued traveling down the academic yellow brick road, moving on to a Visiting Scholar position at USC, I also kept one foot in the world of porn. My insights on PVV developed, as did my understanding of the adult industry, and I continued publishing rigorous scholarly research. But I could feel myself shifting. Though my teaching work as a professor and my research work as a scholar were desperately needed in academia, I could feel it making a greater impact in the everyday world. What once seemed so compelling—scholarship and a university life—gave way to what was truly necessary: social justice for the adult community. I began taking active steps toward these ends. Not surprisingly, a number of representatives from the world of academia had some mixed feelings.

For example, in 2012, I began doing something innovative at AEE. Every year, AEE holds educational seminars alongside their fan days and business activities. The topics of these seminars can range from legal issues shaping the adult business to technology trends and retail strategies. And for the 2012 show, I had the honor of organizing and moderating a panel on women working in porn.

I took the planning and organizing of my panel very seriously, and I wanted it to incorporate two things. First, I wanted a good balance of occupations, not an over-representation of any one dimension. This panel was supposed to be about women working in the industry, and though I knew I couldn't get at every aspect (I was limited to five speakers), I wanted to capture as full a picture as possible. Second, I wanted to have industry leaders involved. Because though everyone at every level certainly has a great deal to contribute, I imagined that people attending this panel wanted to learn something. I figured that the best place to learn was from people who had done it—and had done it well.

So after some shuffling and scheduling and pulling personal favors, my "It's (not) a Man's World: Women Leaders in the Adult Production and Novelty Industry" AEE panel included an incredible fierce five: a woman who was a high-profile performer turned writer and director; a woman executive with a background in marketing and sales who ran production at a major studio; a woman who worked as a sales representative and retail educator for a leading novelty company; the CEO of a leading web-based, tech-centered adult content producer; and an industry reporter who also ran her own boutique public relations firm catering to adult novelty clients. It was amazing. The room was packed. I was on adrenaline fire, and people seemed to love the panel.

There was just one hiccup.

At some point, a woman toward the back of the room raised her hand. After waiting her turn, she asked a statement-question along these lines: "This panel is very nice, but it doesn't really reflect the diversity of the industry, does it?" My heart sank. Because in one painfully obvious respect, she was completely correct. Everyone on the panel was white (and blonde), and the lack of racial diversity was exactly what she was getting at. I knew it, and I had been agonizing over this since the moment I began assembling the panel. Luckily, I'd already thought long and hard about race, diversity, and representation within the context of the event, so I was able to respond with something along the lines of: "Well, if you only focus on physical appearance and the social construction of race to define diversity, then you're completely correct."

I continued, "There are only white people on this panel, and the industry is definitely made up of way more than just white folks. However, I was focusing on occupational diversity when I developed and organized this event. And though there's no way to represent every possible job on a five-person panel, and though I certainly don't know, nor could I ask for a favor from, every woman who works in a specific job—because taking the time out from a business event to sit on this panel is definitely a favor these women are doing for me and for all of us—in terms of women's jobs in adult, this panel is as diverse as possible."

And then the conversation moved on.

It was a perfectly reasonable question, one I had already considered at length. Truth be told, I think about race, class, and gender in everything I do. I had also pondered the same issue in terms of religious and spiritual beliefs and sexual orientation. And though I hadn't asked the panelists about their prayer practices or whom they liked having sex with, I was pretty sure they weren't diverse in those respects either. Throughout the planning process, I had to make decisions based on my two primary goals for the panel, within the context of my resource pool (which relied on my reputation and drew from the personal contacts I had cultivated up to that point). I could have had more women of color on the panel; but replacing a panelist with token diversity at the expense of occupational variety and industry experience, which is what would have happened given my network at the time, would have been a disservice to the entire event. And even though no one else seemed to notice this little blip (with the exception of the questioner herself, who actually apologized to me after the panel had concluded), I agonized over it to the point of doing a little poking around on the Internet.

Thanks to peoples' endless desire to over-share on public digital forums, I discovered that the woman who had asked the question about racial diversity was actually "asking for a friend." One of her associates, a women's studies professor at a large state university, who was also present at the panel, had made some comment about the panel's lack of diversity at the very beginning of the event.

From the perspective of average people living daily lives, querying diversity on racial grounds is more than fair. In fact, I would argue that we as a culture have been programmed to see nothing but race when we think about diversity in general. Further, I would offer that, had I known every single woman who worked in the adult industry such that I could implore them to speak on a panel and I still ended up with a table full of white ladies . . . well *that* would have indicated significant issues related to race and occupational diversity for sure.

But that's not what happened.

For another academic, especially one trained in women's studies and presumably social justice and feminist scholarship to make such an uninformed and uncritical statement, all while watching from the audience and contributing nothing, well, at first I was floored. And mad. Actually, I was furious. But then it made me realize—this was simply one star in the night sky. It was just one of many instances where academics refuse to "see" the adult industry, which indicates an almost canonized refusal to acknowledge the multidimensional quality of human beings and human society as a whole.

My AEE panel in 2012 crystallized something I'd actually known since my early days at CSUN. The conventional path was not for me. The conventional graduate school experience hadn't been mine, and it was clear that a conventional academic career wouldn't be mine either. I was going to have to figure out a new way to be the change I wanted to see in the world, a new way to make the world safer and more inclusive for folks who weren't "normal"—from all those pornographers to so many others just like them. Myself included.

So that's what I'm doing now.

Afterword

NO STORY EVER REALLY ENDS, BUT WHEN ONE REACHES the cutoff point for any big project, it's only natural to sit back and consider everything collectively, as a whole. And when one reflects on the stories in this book, some questions emerge: What does it all mean? What are the takeaways? What are my "conclusions"?

By now, some of the memories shaping these stories are fifteen years old. Some of them are even older. But they all still inform me. They still shape me, and they will always be a part of who I am—and I really like who I am. On a personal level, that's what all this means to me, today. In addition to the personal though, and in addition to the generally obvious (for example, *Don't be an asshole* or *Dr. Chauntelle thinks certain porn movies named here are really good*), there are many broad lessons we can cull from these tales of socio-porno exploration.

First and foremost, society is made up of a vast array of communities and experiences—and though you don't have to like them all, all of them are significant pieces comprising the whole of humanity. As such, all of them are worthy of respectful consideration. Further, whether it concerns the content of a film or a trip to Las Vegas, no two people will ever experience the same thing in the same way. And though we all technically "know" this, the trick is to remain mindful of that fact. Another trick to strive for is the balance between critical (when necessary) and empowering (wherever possible)—no one needs a constant killjoy or a total hater, and a tendency to only identify and/or focus on the negative helps no one.

Finally, there is no authority more correct than your own informed perspective. Every single one of us is human, thus subjective and biased. And though insights and contributions from others are a significant part of what makes the world go 'round, no amount of education or degrees can ever rid an individual of bias. Consequently, you must consider the source and the motives guiding every situation, every insight, and every piece of advice.

When I first began this work, my desires to needle people and push social boundaries were significant motivating factors. (Let's be honest: They were the *biggest* motivating factors.) But as time passed and I grew as a person, both from learning about the adult community and maturing as a human, my endeavors became more about uplifting social justice than anything else—social justice for a community of people who are ultimately no different from you or me. It's ironic, though, that my work seemed to become more irksome to the powers that be as its true purpose shifted to something that was allegedly more in-line with what a large measure of scholarship seeks to achieve.

I've been asked many times, in many different ways, whether, if I knew then what I know now, I would do anything differently in terms of my academic arc. And though I honestly didn't have anything close to a clear concept of how difficult this journey would be at the outset, I can tell you without hesitation that I'd do it all over again.

Sure, knowing how insurmountable my endeavors would occasionally seem might have been helpful. But knowing that the same ridiculous social and institutional bulwarks would be present, no matter who or what I was, well, that might have helped even more. At least then I would have known my presence within this entire series of difficulties was more incidental than consequential. Our world behaves toward porn the way it behaves toward porn, regardless of my presence or involvement. Perhaps understanding this inevitability would simply have made me push harder, sooner. Had I embraced earlier what was ultimately happening anyway, maybe my quest to change the world would be further along.

Which brings me to my even grander, loftier takeaway point for you, dear reader. Fight. Push. And, if your intentions are even remotely pure, don't worry about what other people say. Our larger social institutions are invested in the status quo, as the status quo is what ensures their continued survival. There are many different ways to topple the system, all at once and bit by bit, and there are many different systems that need shaking up. And sometimes, just the idea of fucking with someone or something makes said shake-ups alluring. (At least, it does for me.) But if you're as lucky as I've been—so lucky as to stumble upon a puzzle that truly moves you, for the better—then fight to solve it. And don't give up. Change will eventually come, I promise.

Author's Note

THERE ARE SEVERAL PILLARS WHO HAVE ANCHORED AND shaped me throughout various stages of this process—BCFJ; my parents and brothers; inspirational women MMC, Joy King, AIR, and Jane Prather; my FAM fam, especially Adella and Chris; and my team at Greenleaf, who were able to see *Exposure*, rather than the exposé everyone else seemed to want. Thank you, each and every one.

I would be remiss if did not also mention Christal, Nanciful, LBQ, CER, JZ, Jacky, Lydia, Tracey, Patricia, Asha, Diana, Hailey, DEC, and Nate—the dearest of friends who have put up with my nonsense for a long, long (long) time—as well as RB and TJ for making everything fun, always. Many thanks are also due AVN, XBIZ, IAFD (without which, I could do nothing), the Gender and Sexuality Center at UT, the Sociology Department at CSUN (2000–2003), FSC, YNOT, TRPWL, and Adult DVD Empire. I am grateful for mentorship, friendship, and leadership from Gram Ponante, Angie and Colin Rowntree, Steve Orenstein, Mark Kernes, Brian Alexander, Dan O'Connell and Moose, Ken Herskovitz, Don Houston, Lynn Swanson, Kerry Ferris, Karen Tynan, Allison Vivas, Theresa Flynt, Barbara Collins, and Christian Mann, who will always be here to remind me of the difference a single life can make.

And there are so many more, thousands more. Over the years, there have been so many kind and brilliant people who have helped me in countless huge and/or subtle ways. Some, I'm still in daily contact with, but others have moved on or away, out of the adult industry, sociology, and/or my consciousness. This, however, in no way renders their part in this process any less significant, and I never want to forget. Thus, rather than continuing this litany of name-drops: If we've ever communicated, spoken or otherwise, thank you. You have helped shape my thinking in a meaningful way. If you've ever inspired me, directly or by proxy of your own unique badassery, thank you. You, too, have helped shape my thinking in a meaningful way. And if you've ever looked at me or my work and wondered some form of "What the hell? No."—well, I actually thank you most of all.

—CT

Notes

Chapter 1. How Did a Nice Girl Like You Get into (Studying) Porn?

1. My understanding of *habitus* comes from Pierre Bourdieu's *Distinction* (1984). Habitus is basically your taste—your likes and dislikes and what feels "normal" to you. Your ideas about what's a good joke and what sounds fun to do on a Friday night are part of your habitus, among many other things.

   Habitus develops over time and, thus, may change. Your favorite music as a kid might not be the same when you're a teen. You may be an adventurous low-budget traveler in your twenties, but in your thirties you may want a guided tour and a nice hotel. Habitus also has a social component in the sense that taste can be a marker of social class. For example, a preferred snack of pretzels and beer says something different than a preferred snack of hummus and kombucha. Kicking back and watching TV in your free time says something different than volunteering at an animal shelter (assuming you have free time in the first place).

   In academic speak, habitus is isomorphic to the social structural conditions in which it emerges. It matches where it comes from. So although it can change and develop over time, individual habitus marks and places a person within the context of wider society, including social hierarchies. This part of habitus is not objective or nice, but it does exist in the world we've created.

In the context of the wider society, my habitus is not exactly "classy." This caused a lot of problems for me in graduate school, a space that fancies itself as very classy indeed.

2. Methods and methodology are a significant in any sort of research, and all researchers should be forthcoming with whatever it is that they did to determine their findings. This is important for at least two reasons. First, it lets others possibly replicate a study. Second, it lets people know exactly where your work is coming from. Not sharing a sampling frame (and similar failings in disclosure) or making sweeping generalizations on the basis of unrepresentative data, for example, are indicative of poor scholarship. These things are also antithetical to feminist-informed research principles.

3. Ethnography is like people-watching with a plan. The goal is to watch long enough and often enough such that you can figure out the meanings of ordinary activities. An ethnographer watches, sometimes gets involved (this is called participant observation), and always takes lots of notes. Eventually, they may be able to figure out some patterns.

   For my master's thesis at CSUN, I watched and waited tables in two restaurants: one super corporate and one family owned and informal. I wrote up some of my findings in "Doing Gender as Resistance: Waitresses and Servers in Contemporary Table Service" in the *Journal of Contemporary Ethnography* (2007, volume 36).

4. Funding can make or break a graduate student very quickly. For most programs at top-level research universities, a funding package consists of a full tuition waiver; a teaching assistant (TA) or research assistant (RA) position, which comes with a monthly stipend (which varies by region and program, but it was about $1,400

per month when I was in graduate school at UT); full health insurance benefits; office space; and office perks (printing, copying, supplies, etc).

Departmental funding is based on evaluations of students by faculty. Supposedly, faculty assess students' progress annually through the duration of the program, but their actual assessments and the ins and outs of the process are kept private. Students do not get to see how they are being evaluated, nor are they given feedback to make improvements. Further, professors are asked to state how well they know an individual student at the outset of each assessment. A professor's assessment is then weighted on the basis of the perceived student-teacher relationship. Assessments from professors who claim to know students more closely are given greater weight, so students are advised to make good impressions on key faculty.

Without funding, or at least an in-state tuition waiver (which drops your tuition rate considerably), a graduate student's costs add up quickly.

During my time at UT, a full term of units, which you must be enrolled in every semester regardless of whether you were actually taking classes (while writing your dissertation, you can enroll in "dissertation hours," which are basically space-keeper units and involve no actual class time but cost the same), cost approximately $3,000 for in-state tuition and $6,000 for out-of-state tuition. It took me six total years (or twelve semesters) to complete my PhD, and I lost my funding after my first year. Because I was not from Texas, unless I managed to secure some form of external funding, I had to pay tuition at the out-of-state rate.

5. The following summarizes my two hundred-plus-page dissertation project. Enjoy!

Women work in the adult industry as performers *and* in a variety of behind-the-scenes occupations and executive roles. But, as would be expected, women were not always integrated into every level of the adult industry. The process of integration occurred over time, just as it did in myriad other workplaces; however, unlike many other workplaces, neither advocacy from an external social movement nor activism from workers within the industry initiated this integration. My dissertation research explored the following two questions: First, how has women's incorporation and opportunities for participation in the United States' adult film industry changed since the 1950s? Second, how has the content of adult films changed since the 1950s?

The evidence I found suggested that women's labor incorporation and opportunities for participation expanded internally, from the top down. Company owners, film producers, and powerful industry leaders began expanding women's rights, and thus, partially, their incorporation into the workplace, in response to legal and cultural pressures from regulators and industry-wide structural changes occurring during the late 1970s and early 1980s.

Regarding the processes responsible for these developments: In a nutshell, the development of the adult industry over the years has been shaped by dynamic multidimensional tensions among producers, consumers, and regulators. These tensions are partially reflected in the content of key adult films. The historical development of the industry has led to the emergence of a closely interconnected occupational network. This network and what I call "industry protective practices"—endeavors initiated by adult industry business leaders, owners, and producers that protect both the welfare of workers and the industry itself—operate synergistically and are responsible for the top-down expansion of women workers' labor rights and opportunities over time. Industry leaders and business owners employ industry protective practices to sustain the social network and as strategic measures to avoid regulation and scrutiny from entities outside the adult industry.

6. "Writing grants" are exactly what they sound like: sizable chunks of money intended to support a student who is writing up research. Students with a substantial writing grant may spend their days overwhelmed by the task at hand and/or freaking out about a life that often feels both out-of-control and directionless; but ultimately, all they have to do is . . . type.

Chapter 3. Watching Porn for Science

1. See my work "From *The Devil in Miss Jones* to *DMJ6*: Power, Inequality, and Consistency in the Content of US Adult Films" in *Sexualities* 13 (2010) for a detailed rendering of this entire study.

Chapter 4. Working the Booth

1. RealDolls are designed to mimic the appearance, texture, and weight of the human form. An average RealDoll costs about $6,000 and is completely customizable, with a pose-able PVC skeleton and silicone flesh. They require regular maintenance and upkeep.

A doll's primary function is to serve as its owner's sex partner; however, these ladies are so real that they often work their way into a person's entire life, psyche, and emotions. RealDolls often become companions.

Chapter 8. Academic Snubbery

1. At the time, in the sociology department at UT, $500 was the maximum annual travel allowance for graduate students.

Chapter 9. The Slippery Slope of Subjectivity

1. E-mail correspondence, quoted with permission.

Chapter 10. "Tranny," Queer, and Tales of Loaded Language

1. Passage quoted from early versions of my work "Gonzo, Trannys, and Teens—Current Trends in United States' Adult Content Production, Distribution, and Consumption" in *Porn Studies* 1, no. 1–2 (2014).

2. First named by legal scholar Kimberlé Crenshaw, intersectionality is the study of the intersections occurring between wider social systems of oppression, domination, and discrimination. For example, in black feminist theory, it is understood that experiences of race and gender are not independent, thus should not be considered as such. What happens at the junctures between race and gender (as well as any combination of age, ethnicity, able-bodiedness, sexual orientation, global positionality, social class, etc.) is unique, often synergistic, and always significant.

3. See note 1 for reference.

4. E-mail correspondence, quoted with permission.

5. It's worth noting that the "Tranny Awards" are now known as the Transgender Erotica Awards (or, the TEAs). Organizers Grooby Entertainment changed the name in early 2014 for the event's seventh annual gala. According to Grooby Entertainment CEO Steven Grooby (via press release), the original name was no longer appropriate. "Tranny" had ceased to convey the lighthearted tenor they had originally intended and was insufficiently inclusive.

   In terms of sociology and social justice, I confess that I was really, really happy when I learned about this name change. Plus the TEAs—which is a fun play on the T in LGBTQ and the word "tease," as in a sexy tease—is super cute!

Chapter 11. Pegging: The Oldest New Trick in the Book

1. See Chapter 3, note 1.

2. Heteronormativity is a worldview that promotes heterosexuality as the "normal" or preferred sexual orientation.

Chapter 12. Beyond Porn Funk

1. Jean Baudrillard's *Simulacra and Simulation* (1981) calls the relationships existing among and between reality, symbols, and society into question. Simulacra are copies (of copies of copies, etc.) that depict things that either had no reality to begin with or that no longer have an original. Baudrillard discusses casinos in Las Vegas as the ultimate simulacra—imitations of cities (for example, New York or Paris) that reflect a popular imagination of what something is or was, versus what actually is or may have been.

   People's *bow-chicka-bow-wow*ing of porn is a simulacrum, both of adult content (classic and contemporary) as well as funk music in general.

Chapter 14. Being a Guy in Porn Is (Not) Hard

1. A mope is a low-prestige class of adult performer. Mopes generally add numbers to large gangbang scenes and are very rarely credited beyond "Guy #X," etc.

Chapter 15. *Match Mates*

1. Gonzo is a film form that incorporates the use of a "talking camera," where the person capturing a particular sequence or scene is also playing an active, integral role in the on-screen action. For example, in porn, a person may be holding the camera while giving directions or making comments to people performing in a sex scene. Gonzo form content can be found in all genres and sub-genres of porn.

2. You may be wondering why I'm masking Kelle's and Ms. X's identities here, but not Manuel's. Well, pretty much every performer I know wants to work with Manuel Ferrara, for the first time or the tenth. And he works all the time. So though Kelle is both singular and special, her lust for Manuel is not. In this respect, she could be anyone.

Chapter 16. The Real Linda Lovelace (née Boreman, née Marchiano)

1. See "The Real Linda Lovelace" in Gloria Steinem's collection *Outrageous Acts and Everyday Rebellions,* 2nd edition (1995). This volume also contains the essay "Erotica vs. Pornography," which was integral to my formative thinking about porn.

2. *Ordeal* (1980) is the third in a series of publications listing Linda Lovelace as their author. Linda had previously published the (alleged) autobiographies *Inside Linda Lovelace* (1973) and *The Intimate Diary of Linda Lovelace* (1974). Compared to *Ordeal* and the subsequent *Out Of Bondage* (1986), these earlier texts are remarkably different in content and tone. Linda claimed Chuck Traynor was responsible for shaping the first two books, using her name and persona without her approval.

Chapter 17. Sexuality Through the Ages

1. A star showcase is a title made up of a collection of new content, a diverse set of scenes with a particular performer "showcased" in each. *Meet Bonnie Rotten* (2012), for example, included Bonnie in two boy-girl scenes (one anal), an all-girl three-way with toys, and a boy-boy-girl double-penetration scene. Interview sequences with the star being showcased generally happen between each scene.

2. See Chapter 10, note 1.

Chapter 20. Coming Out Porno

1. Do you know what a *cum fart* is? Put simply, it's what may happen when a person who has just had anal sex starts moving around. Air inevitably gets into various bodily cavities during the process and must come out. Mix that expulsion with fluids that may have been introduced during the scene, and what you get is a squishy, noisy, but ultimately innocuous cum fart.

2. See my work "Adult Performers and Occupational Safety and Health" in *Stanford Law and Policy Review* (*SLPR*) 23 (2013).

About the Author

CHAUNTELLE TIBBALS, PHD, is a sociologist specializing in gender, sexualities, work and organizations, and media and popular culture. She earned her PhD from the University of Texas at Austin (UT) in 2010 and was a Visiting Scholar in the University of Southern California's (USC) Department of Sociology from 2012 to 2013.

Dr. Chauntelle has spent more than ten years researching the adult entertainment industry, working to complicate popular understandings of pornography, its enterprise, and its sociocultural significance. Her research has been published in numerous scholarly journals, including *Stanford Law and Policy Review* and *Gender, Work & Organization*; her essays and op-eds have appeared in popular periodicals, including *Men's Health* and *Playboy*; and, she has been quoted and cited in news outlets, including Huffington Post, Al Jazeera, and CNN.

Dr. Chauntelle was born and raised in Los Angeles, California, where she lives today.

For more information, see ChauntelleTibbals.com and visit her on Twitter at @drchauntelle.

Made in the USA
San Bernardino, CA
04 October 2017